A *Lakes* CHRISTMAS

Compiled by

SHEILA RICHARDSON

ALAN SUTTON

First published in the United Kingdom in 1991
Alan Sutton Publishing Limited · Phoenix Mill
Far Thrupp · Stroud · Gloucestershire

First published in the United States of America in 1991
Alan Sutton Publishing Inc · Wolfeboro Falls
NH 03896–0848

British Library Cataloguing in Publication Data

Richardson, Sheila, *1935–*
A Lakes Christmas.
I. Title
820.8033

ISBN 0-86299-921-9

Cover illustration:
Winter Skating Scene, *Fine Art Photographic Library Limited.*

Typeset in Garamond 12/13
Typesetting and origination by
Alan Sutton Publishing Limited.
Printed in Great Britain by
The Bath Press, Avon.

The Twelve Days of Yule

DOROTHY UNA RATCLIFFE

Dorothy Una Ratcliffe was the pen name of Mrs McGrigor Phillips who came from Yorkshire to live at Temple Sowerby Manor in 1930 with her husband, Captain McGrigor Phillips.

She was a writer of North Country prose and verse. A newspaper article of 1937 tells, 'Her prose has all the imagery of poetry, and she can paint pictures in colourful words as an artist can paint them in pigment'.

Both she and her husband were interested in wildlife and natural history and established a bird sanctuary and a wild flower reserve in the extensive gardens of their home. D.U.R., as she was often referred to, drew on her background knowledge of natural history for much of her writing. At one time, she was President of the Penrith Natural History Society.

Another newspaper article explained, 'A kindly fate endowed her with a lot of this world's wealth, but the good fairies of Yorkshire also blessed Miss Dorothy with an abundance of common sense, humility, sympathy and a love of beautiful things which has increased as she has lived'.

In 1950 Temple Sowerby Manor, which is situated in

the Eden Valley, along with its extensive gardens, was presented to the National Trust. It reverted to its former name of Acorn Bank. D.U.R. moved to the Borders area where she died in 1967. The house, Acorn Bank, is now let to the Sue Ryder foundation, but the gardens are open to members of the public.

The first day of Yule, I gave my dearest dear
Sprigs of berried hollins from a bush at Buttermere.
The second day of Yule, from Borrowdale's lone fells
We heard down the valley, the chimes of far-off bells.
The third day of Yule, where children's voices rang
Besides the banks of Rydal, a robin bravely sang.
The fourth day of Yule, my dearest dear gave me
A shepherd's crook from Caldbeck, made from a hazel tree.
The fifth night of Yule, we saw the Northern Lights

Langdale Pikes in Winter

· A Lakes Christmas ·

Playing over Pavey Ark – greens and pearly whites.
The sixth night of Yule, below the Langdale Pikes
A bright eyed fox was drinking in one of Stickle's sikes.
The seventh day of Yule, we came down Striding Edge
Then watched the falling waters under Aira bridge.
The eighth day of Yule, a watchful heron flew
Along the pass of Honister to a sanctuary he knew.
The ninth day of Yule, on the way to Dunmail Raise
We heard folk in the little kirk singing psalms of praise.
The tenth day of Yule, up on Hard Knott Pass
A flock of Herdwicks nibbled among the sweet, short grass.
The eleventh day of Yule, just below Blea Tarn
We sheltered from a dark blue storm inside a weathered barn.
The twelveth day of Yule, on Glaramara side
My dearest dear learned that I would love her till I died.

Passage over Dunmail Raise, 1909

Wainwright

The creator of the popular Lake District Pictorial Guides,
A. Wainwright, used the long winter nights to recreate
the detailed black and white drawings and carefully
printed script from photographs and notes taken during
preparatory field work, and the Christmas break from his
work as Borough Treasurer in Kendal gave him the
opportunity to write up the Personal Notes that conclude
three of the seven volumns of the Lakeland Guides. *The*
beauty of the lakes in winter made a vivid impression on
his memory, for in his book Ex-Fellwanderer, *he recalled*
the winter of 1963 – 64.

. . . The district was gripped by a severe frost for three months
without respite, the lakes were sheets of ice and the fells
encased in frozen snow. The conditions put paid to fell
walking. But the scenery was very beautiful. Borrowdale,
which I visited every Sunday, was transformed into a fairyland
of exquisite charm, a delicate tracery of black and white. I was
entranced. This was a new Lakeland. Even without colour it
was the loveliest place on earth.

While A.W. appreciated the beauty that snow and ice
brought to the landscape, he was also aware of the dangers
that they presented. In his earlier book, Fellwanderer, *he*
wrote,

Snow is a more subtle adversary. It transforms the fells into

The late A. Wainwright at his Kendal home

fields of dazzling whiteness and the distant scene into a fairy wonderland. It is beautiful, beautiful, but treacherous. Snow is feminine, a temptress; when you meet her, watch your step. When her seduction hardens into ice, avoid her.

> *An extract from the concluding notes to Book Seven, the last of his Pictorial Guides, could be read as the nearest that A.W. came to sending a Christmas greeting to the many thousands of his readers.*

The fleeting hour of life of those who love the hills is quickly spent, but the hills are eternal. Always there will be the lonely ridge, the dancing beck, the silent forest; always there will be the exhilaration of summits. These are for the seeking, and those who seek and find while there is yet time, will be blessed in both mind and body. I wish you all many happy days on the

Great Gable and Green Gable from track to Esk Hause

6

fells in the years ahead. There will be fair winds and foul, days of sun and rain. But enjoy them all.

Good walking. And don't forget – watch where you are putting your feet.

Christmas 1965 A.W.

Keswick's Victorian Christmas Fair

Christmas gets under way in the Lake District town of Keswick with the holding of a 'Victorian Fair'. It is organized by the town's Chamber of Trade and Commerce with the dual purpose of providing financial backing for the Christmas lights that decorate the streets, and also to give local charities the opportunity to raise much needed funds to support their individual ventures.

The Fair is held on an early Sunday in December and is a popular family day out, not only for the people of Keswick, but also for others who live much further afield.

What's that? You can't make it? Never mind, come and have a look round now.

The Fair is held in the Main Street of Keswick, in the area known as the Market Place. Over the years, this has been used for many different purposes – bull-baiting, cock-fighting, the hiring of labour, wool trading as well as the more traditional market activities. The Blencathra foxhounds meet in this area before setting off on their annual Boxing Day Hunt.

The old Moot Hall, which was once a prison, stands as a grey division between the activities of the Victorian Fair. With its overtones of nostalgia alongside the colourful blaze of flashing roundabout lights from the rides that are there to entertain twentieth-century youngsters, there is something for everyone to enjoy. Local people are encouraged to don Victorian costume to give an air of authenticity to the scene, and it is rather odd being served in a modern store by a young lass in long dress and mob cap – a curious mixture of old and new. There is a greater sense of realism out in the market place where men in top hats and frock coats, and ladies in long skirts and bonnets, mingle with the crowd.

People gather round the band at the Victorian Fair,
Keswick, December, 1990

· A Lakes Christmas ·

Noise, colour, and smells invade the senses. A brass band with brightly shining instruments reflecting coloured lights, actually plays tunes with recognizable melodies which set the feet tapping. Stalls along the streets sell mince pies and hot mulled wine; their spicy scent drifts into nostrils chilled by cold, reminding one of Christmas long ago. It comes as something of a mental jolt to have helpings of steaming wine served in modern polystyrene cups. Another stall emits the hot, floury smell of jacket potatoes, finger burning, but once again served in the plastic packing of our times. At least the stall holders look the part as they face the reaching hands of bargain hunters to get at the jumble, while the home baking rapidly disappears to the welcome chink of coins, like the proverbial 'snow off a dyke'. Even the local constabulary enter into the spirit of the day. Two officers in buttoned up tunics and caps mingle with the good humoured crowd. They are frequently asked if they are 'the real thing', and when asked if they administer Victorian justice, only reply with a wink.

A group of Morris men provide action and colour. Hankies wave and leg bells tinkle as they follow the intricacies of the dance, leaping high with light-footed step. Reds and greens swirl in a moving circle as hat streamers flow with the speed of the dance. The group, which performs at many locations, is the Cumberland Morris Men, formed about fourteen years ago. The majority of their members come from West Cumbria, and while most of their dances are Cotswold in origin, they also perform traditional Border dances.

At the Keswick Victorian Fair they break with tradition and dance to the music of carols, rather than the more usual Morris tunes. A ladies dance group also entertains the crowds with some Cumbrian dances, one of which is the Wigton Carnival Dance. Apparently there is difficulty in obtaining old Cumbrian dance routines, for most of the steps and sequences were handed down through the generations by practice and word of mouth, and were not recorded in a printed form. As old customs have died out, so has the knowledge of the traditional dance steps, and this group, the Belfagan, also West Cumbrian based, use dances that originate from the Lancashire mills to complete their programme.

As the dances end, the reedy music of accordion and concertina is replaced by the strident tones of a Dutch street organ which accompanies its moving figures and flashing lights, to provide moments of magic for wide-eyed youngsters. The street entertainment continues with a Punch and Judy show that has more children screaming for Mr Punch, dodging the whirling sausages as they draw close to the centre of the action. They huddle, tight-packed and wide-eyed, round the candy striped tent while in the background, parents sip the mulled wine, hot, spicy and good. The Moot Hall is a welcome haven of escape from the good natured jostle of the crowds, for in the upper room is the opportunity to sit down and enjoy a cup of coffee and the inevitable mince pie. The 'Victorian' ladies, organizers of the Fair, have lost count of the number of coffees served, and pies consumed, as they try to catch a quiet moment to rest. After all, they have been on the go since early morning. 'Don't forget to visit Santa's Grotto,' they call out to those refreshed once more, and up a further flight of stairs, there he is, Father Christmas, and Mother Christmas with him.

Late in the day, they have almost run out of presents for the still queuing youngsters, but the red gown and white whiskers combined with that special secret whisper in the ear give that shared confidence the reassurance that come 'The Day' all will be well.

Outside the sky has darkened, the Christmas lights strung across the streets shine bright, and gaily lit windows of shops give a sense of warmth. The crowd gathers round the band in cosy friendliness as old familiar carols ring round the grey, stone place, enveloping everyone in warm good humour. There is music, light, colour; good-natured jostling, friendly

faces and chatter as the crowd draws ever closer. 'Hark the Herald Angels sing' – Christmas has begun.

from

Months at the Lakes

REVD H.D. RAWNSLEY

Canon Rawnsley was one of the three founders of the National Trust. He was a prolific writer on the natural history, folk lore and customs, and history of the lakes area. He was a champion of local causes, and in those far off days of the late nineteenth century was aware of the pressure that the Lake District would be subjected to due to the development of a tourist industry.

Between 1886 and 1906 he kept a monthly record of the changes that he saw in the natural history of the area, and also the 'noticeable goings on' of the valley people. The following extracts are taken from his book, Months at the Lakes.

There are few months more variable in mood and character than December at the lakes. At times it is a month of storm and wind . . . at others we have windless calm and our lakes lie like mirrors for Father Christmas or the glad New Year to see their faces in; . . .

11

· *A Lakes Christmas* ·

Winter at Crosthwaite – Canon Rawnsley was Vicar of
Crosthwaite for many years

The charm of the woodland at this time of year lies in the
ruddy hue of the fallen leaf and the faded bracken on the
ground, and the little russet-coated squirrel that sits up alone
and regales himself between his slumbers with beech mast and
pine cone seed. But the beauty of the wood is much enhanced
by the noble growth of the holly.

Hollies grow in the lake country if they escape the
woodman's axe, as if the lake country was peculiarly their own,
and though the time is past when the shepherds of Furness
Abbey, to provide the Abbot with a Christmas delicacy, fed
their flocks on the holly boughs in the winter months, and
though there are no Druids left to give a special sanctity to the
tree, still wherever the holly can grow, it will grow and
nothing is more beautiful than the green oases in our winter
woodlands made by the sunlit holly tree . . .

Christmastide time out of mind has been a time of great

festivity. There is still a general feeling that work shall cease on Christmas Day and not be done save in a desultory manner until well into the New Year. The old custom of the 'Merrie Neet' has largely ceased to be. In old days one felt almost honour bound if one was a dalesman, to go off to the public-house of the vale as a guest at such a merry night . . . they were pleasant gatherings of friends when master and man and mistress and girl met on frank and open terms, and enjoyed a crack and a dance or a game of whist to their heart's content. . . .

On the main hearth of the public-house, as indeed in the kitchens of most farmhouses, a yule-log was alight. I have spoken with old men who remember the taking into the farm kitchen of whole trees whose lighted end was on the hearth and once alight was not allowed to be extinguished until the tree had been consumed. In the little chapel of Newlands it was the duty of the clerk to see that such a yule-log was procured for Sunday use, and the log after having done duty at the service was handed out into the open and kept till the following Sunday called its services again into requisition. . . .

Boys went round the whole of a dale with a fiddler, who at each house they came to, called out the name of master and mistress and played them a tune and wished them Merry Christmas.

Then the sons' names and the daughters' names were called and another tune was played, then the servant man, or maid was called and the tune repeated and more good wishes given. The family had generally retired to rest, but they rose up at the sound of the fiddle, put their heads out of the window, and returned the Christmas greetings. The fiddler was repaid for his pilgrimage at the Merrie Neet on some succeeding night, though very often cakes and a jug of beer were standing outside the door to be partaken of by all who came. The fiddler has ceased to be, but carol singers in different parts of the lake country carry on the custom of awakening the night with music, whilst one custom has not ceased, and that is the friendly card party at the various farmhouses. The dalesmen are great players of whist; I have heard of a whist party that began on Christmas Eve and owing to a heavy fall of snow preventing the departing of the guests, went on for forty-eight hours at a stretch.

Generally speaking, the feeling for Christmas holiday is as strong as it is wide-spread in expression. The old Norse feeling for Yule as a time for rejoicing at the Winter solstice and the return of the sun has never died. . . .

Wordsworth wrote of the custom of the fiddler going round the valleys – it was included in a selection of sonnets to the river Duddon, and quoted by Rawnsley.

The minstrels played their Christmas tune
Tonight beneath my cottage eaves;
While, smitten by a lofty moon,
The encircling laurels, thick with leaves,
Gave back a rich and dazzling sheen,
That overpowered their natural green.

Through hill and valley every breeze
Had sunk to rest with folded wings;
Keen was the air, but could not freeze,
Nor check, the music of the strings;
So stout and hardy were the band
That scraped the chords with strenuous hand;

And who but listened? – till was paid
Respect to every Inmate's claim;
The greeting given, the music played,
In honour of each household name,
Duly pronounced with lusty call.
And 'merry Christmas' wished to all.

Monday morning was the Keswick Hunt – an institution that is as important as any custom in the dale. At 9.30 the wanderer in our midst would have been astonished to find the Market Place filled with men and boys, armed with their mountain staves, and with their lunch bulging in their pockets. . . .

I heard a horn, and saw coming round the Royal Oak corner the red-coated huntsman, with the hounds twinkling at his heels. How all the lads rushed to meet him, and how imperturbably he and his hounds came on, through the welcoming crowd, into the Market Square. Then, waving his whip to give his beauties space, he shook hands with the Master of the Hunt, and got his instructions for the day. But what, we cannot begin the day's 'diversion' without 'a la'al bit song'. The hounds must have music wherever they go, and grand music it is, as all know who have heard the side of silent

Skiddaw and Bassenthwaite on a calm winter morning

Skiddaw suddenly find a voice and echo to the mellow chiming of the Blencathra pack. But their time for music has not come; it is ours to make music for them. . . .

And there, in the middle of the ring, with the old Town Hall to be a sounding board and all the houses in the Market Square to echo back the song, Melvin of the sturdy voice strikes up 'D'ye ken John Peel', waves his hands when he gets to the end of the first verse, and with a cry 'Now, all together' obliges the whole crowd – men, women, children, parson, lawyer, banker, tradesman to shout the chorus 'Yes I ken John Peel', till one felt the sound of the chorus would fly over Skiddaw top to the far off Caldbeckdale, and waken from the dead the veteran huntsman who was run to earth fifty years ago.

Then the song ceases. The huntsman winds a blast upon his horn, and away go the dogs, and away at their heels the whole town multitude, for their annual breather upon Skiddaw's side, through the frost and sunshine of a glorious winter morning.

Christmas at the Wasdale Head Inn

1879 – 1894

Four leather bound visitors' books from the Wasdale Head Inn record visits and exploits of climbers of the late nineteenth century, who later became household names

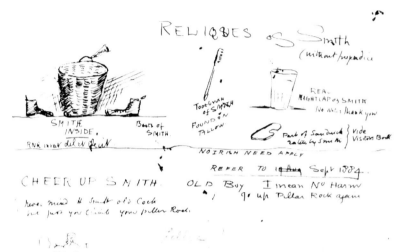

Climbing contemporaries were not always impressed with
Haskett-Smith's achievements, as these cartoons from the
Visitors' Book indicate

*among the rock climbing fraternity of the new sport that
had its birth at Wasdale.*

*It could be said that rock climbing began with Walter
Parry Haskett-Smith's solo ascent of Napes Needle which
he discovered and climbed in 1886. A local man, John
Wilson Robinson of Lorton, near Cockermouth, climbed
many of the now classic routes with him. Both men feature
prominently in the visitors' books, Haskett-Smith being the
butt of many humorous cartoons. Parties of university
students came to stay at the Inn for 'study reading' periods
during their long college holidays. After hours spent with
their books, they would take to the fells and rocks for
physical recreation.*

*The Fell and Rock Climbing Club of the English
Lakes, formed in 1907, had the visitors' books in their
care, until it was felt that they should be deposited with
the County Record Office at Kendal for safe keeping. It is*

with their permission and co-operation that the following extracts are included.

27 December 1881. This entry gives a seasonal recommendation:

Notice to visitors. If you ever come here about Christmas time be sure and ask for a Mince pie, they are splendid about the size of a good big plate.

Almost a year later, on 26 December 1882, Mr and Mrs Martin from Huddersfield:

arrived here from Rosthwaite by Honister Pass over Grey Knotts, Brandreth and Great Gable – dense fog all the way – waited patiently for three days for the fog to clear away.

Three days later, the weather relented, and they recorded the following entry in the visitors' book:

Saturday December 30th Magnificent day – frosty and slight fall of snow on the mountains – ascended by Great Gable by gully between Great Gable and Kirkfell – perfect views on all sides. Descended by Sty Head Tarn and thence ascended Scafell Pikes via Esk Hause views equally grand on all sides. Crossed Mickledore and descended the screes and home by Lingmell.

Few people seemed to visit the Inn during the winter months, although it appeared to be a reception point for all the paraphernalia left lying around on the fells:

Found on the fells
A pole (Piers Gill); a bit of rope; an old basket (Pillar); a spike or two and several walking sticks, including two proudly planted halfway up Pavey Ark just *below* the first real difficulty. Owners may apply at the Inn.
A flat flask of brandy (found on Pillar Rock-East Climb)

Owner may apply at top of Scafell Pillar. (The bottle will be found minus the brandy – anxiously expecting the insertion of its owners, or anyone else's card.)

W.P.H.S.

Throughout the year, there were many references to the quality of the hospitality of the Inn. 'Clean but primitive' was the opinion held by one visitor. Another, E.A. Mayer, found it more to his liking and recorded in verse the qualities of the Inn and the landlord:

Of the Hotel at Wasdale Head
A word of praise is justly said.
You have your supper, stay the night
And then start off at morning light.
Unless perchance a change of weather
Detains you there for days together.
You might go further, fare much worse
And leave with a much lighter purse.
So passing traveller, thankful be
For Tyson's hospitality
For good the food, well aired the bed
At the hotel at Wasdale Head.

From 4–7 January 1887 J.W. Robinson and T.G. Creak used the hotel as a base for climbs on Scafell Pike and Pillar, and on Gable and Scafell. Robinson records in the visitors' book:

Wednesday (Jan 5th) Misty, heavy fall of snow during the night, ascended Scawfell Pikes via Esk Hause. The top of the Pikes a wonderful sight, the few rocks to be seen above the deep snow being completely covered with ice in most fantastic shapes; a glissade of five or six hundred feet from the Mickledore ridge brought us out of the mist into the moon light.

· A Lakes Christmas ·

In 1887, the Inn was busy with visitors over the Christmas period, when there were 15 signatures in the visitors' book. Once again, the combination of snow, ice and rock was the great attraction;

Dec. 30. Three of the party led by Hopkinson made an attempt on the Deep Ghyll Pillar (Pinnacle) from the entrance to Lord's Rake. They succeeded in climbing . . . feet but were stopped by a steep slab of rock coated with ice. From this point however a good traverse was made to the first gully (or chimney) on the left (apparently that referred to by Mr Haskett-Smith). They forced their way up this gully to the top of the chimney. At the top of the chimney there was a trough of ice about 30 ft. long surmounted by steep rocks glazed with ice which brought the party to a stop. They descended the chimney again and returned to Wasdale being unanimously of opinion that the day's excursion had afforded one of the finest climbs the party had ever accomplished.

Dec 31. Three of the party went up Cust's gully but found no difficulty whatever excepting the company of a spotted dog which having persistently followed from Wasdale had to be thrown up the steps, drawing from one member of the party an . . . series of epithets upon the poor beast.

Not all visitors to the Wasdale Head Inn were climbers.
16 December 1890 has the signatures of;

Herbert Lunn – Netherton
Edward Lister – Lockwood
F. Barraclough – Lockwood
Lily Sunderland – Lockwood.
The above are part of Messr.'s Lunns concert party who gave a grand performance at Drigg on Dec 15th/'90 remainder of party got screwed at Seascale and did not arrive here as appointed.

Pen and ink drawing of a Lake District pack horse bridge as an
illustration in the Wasdale Head Inn Visitors' Book, 1892

Smoking was considered an anti-social activity even in those far-off days for there is a heartfelt plea written in the book:

Will the gentlemen who are fond of smoking please remember that there are others who do <u>not</u> enjoy the fumes of their favourite weed and be good enough not to smoke in the house nor just outside the bedroom windows. They would add greatly to the comfort of their fellow travellers.

A Christmas as an Evacuee

JOAN MULLEN

Joan Mullen lives in South Shields, in the county of Tyne and Wear, but whenever possible comes to the Lake District to walk the fells in an area that she came to know through being evacuated here from the bomb-threatened north-eastern England of the Second World War. She tells of her memories of her first Christmas away from home.

Bright moonlight, the smell of oil-lamps, and a sharp nose-tingling crispness in the air; memories came flooding back of my first Christmas as a war-time evacuee in

Cumberland. I became an evacuee, literally, overnight. One day, I was in a shelter listening to the sounds of sirens, explosions and a terrifying air raid which destroyed our home; and the next day I was transported to the wonderful world of Lakeland. To a seven-year-old 'townie' used to nightly bombing raids, it was Shangri-La; and now, here we were preparing for Christmas.

At our village school in Frizington, the headmaster had managed to acquire some crêpe paper (quite a feat in wartime), of two colours, pink and blue. Our class was given the privilege of decorating the school with carefully stretched and crimped paper chains. It was the only artificial decoration used as local trees would supply us with holly, pine cones, acorn cups, and 'pixie hats' from the beech. These were to be carefully collected on a school trip to one of the lakes.

It was with an air of great excitement that we trooped, crocodile style, from the school to board the bus that was to take us to Ennerdale, stopping on the way to collect some pupils from Cleator Moor Junior School, who were to join our little expedition.

The day started very grey and damp, but by the time we had reached our destination a pale, watery sun was breaking through, bathing the lake and surrounding fells in a rosy, ethereal mist. The delicate pastel colours of the sky reflected in the snowshine on the summits. That is when I fell in love totally and completely with this wonderland; a feeling which has steadily increased with the passing years. To a child from the coast on the opposite side of the country, used to the fury of North Sea waves, the calm rippling water of the lake, and magnificence of the fells with their spun-sugar covering of snow on the tops, was fairyland.

The time to return to school came too quickly, and with a last lingering look at the wild beauty of Ennerdale, I boarded the bus along with all the others, our arms full of greenery and

pockets bulging with fir cones. My first lesson in conservation and preserving the countryside was learned that day as we were instructed to collect only the fallen branches, twigs and cones, and to leave all growing things intact.

Back at school great care was taken with the decorations of each classroom and the assembly hall, and it all looked lovely. On the last day of school, before breaking up for the Christmas holidays, we were allowed a special treat with our morning milk – double ration of digestive biscuits. The distribution of the milk itself was quite different to most other schools. Not for us ordinary glass bottles – no, we had beautifully coloured beakers, each one carefully filled from a pitcher of milk that was very often warm from the cow. As there were quite a number of farms in the area, there was no shortage of milk. In fact, it was one of my daily duties to carry a large jug down Main Street to Fearons' farm for two pennyworth of milk. I think it was just before tubercular testing became compulsory, but drinking warm milk freshly 'delivered' didn't appear to harm any of us.

However, it is Christmas itself that remains crystal clear in my memory. Frost rimed the rooftops and sparkled in the moonlight on Christmas Eve. The air was so sharp and cold it stung my nose when breathed in deeply. Everything was silent as I made my way down Main Street to the Wesleyan Chapel, where we children of its Sunday School, attended each week. We were to meet there before going carol singing.

Muffled up to the eyes and with a huge scarf wrapped umpteen times around me, I stood, stamping my feet to keep them warm. I was wearing my new blue clogs with iron corkers which were my pride and joy. It had taken a lot of pleading and persuasion to be allowed to have iron ones instead of rubber. After all, only babies had rubber ones, and I was seven! Now with my iron corkers, I could kick the edge of the pavement and make lovely sparks. Also, walking in the snow with them was quite an acrobatic achievement as the snow collected in a hard ball on the sole of each clog, getting bigger and bigger until it was almost like walking on stilts. This was always a popular game which caused great hilarity at the expense of the first one to 'fall off their clogs'.

When we had all arrived at the little hall, the two Sunday School teachers, each holding an oil lamp, led us to the top of the village street where we started our carol singing. No need for music or song sheets, even if we could have seen them, as everyone knew the words. Our small group gradually made its way down Main Street with childish voices singing lustily, if not always in tune, and augmented by a couple of baritones. The lanterns were no competition at all for the brilliant moon. However, when we were standing in the shadows, their warm light was cosy and welcome.

At the end of the carol singing, a short service was held in the Chapel, and as we were leaving, the resident barn owl swooped so low over our heads I could feel his wings brush my hair. No doubt he had spotted some juciy morsel for supper. Going to bed that night, I looked out of the bedroom window. The velvety blackness of shadowed doorways across the road was accentuated by the brilliance of the moon. Everything was so still and peaceful; only the occasional bleating of a sheep broke the silence. It would soon be Christmas Day.

Christmas morning dawned clear and cold and full of excitement. A shortage of toys and books didn't matter as everyone was in the same situation. Nevertheless there were presents for all the children, and although food was rationed, a goose graced our table – no doubt from one of the neighbouring farms. Sweet coupons must have been saved for weeks by the grown-ups because there was quite a mouth-watering selection in the stocking that I had hung up, hopefully, the evening before. Apples and nuts replaced the traditional orange in the toe. Oranges were extremely scarce during the war years.

· A Lakes Christmas ·

Our neighbours came in to wish us a 'Happy Christmas', and then it was our turn to visit their homes. No door was closed, and all were made welcome. It was a time I remember, when everything was shared; not just during the festive season, but all the time during those war torn years.

Later that day when, full of goose and goodies, I watched the cows ambling down the road back to the farm for milking, protesting noisily at the impatience of the farm dog; had I been granted one wish, it would have been for everything in my little world to stay just as it was. I'd discovered the warmth of friendship and sharing, and although almost half a century has passed since that particular Christmas, the memory of it remains as clear as though it were yesterday.

My childhood was a very happy one, but the three years that I spent as an evacuee in Cumberland were the happiest of all.

Geese in a Cumbrian farmyard

from

To the King's Deceit – A Study in Smuggling on the Solway

RONALD T. GIBBON

During the long hours of darkness of December nights almost two centuries ago, smuggling was rife along the Cumbrian coast. Rum and brandy were important com-modities to add cheer to the Christmas scene, not only as a drink, but also as vital ingredients to festive fare such as rum butter and the 'stannin pies', the recipes for which required at least one good measure of rum; the more the better some might say.

Lower rates of excise duty in the Isle of Man and Scotland encouraged the illegal trade into the county with the support of many local 'worthies'. It was not unknown for the local parson to go home after conducting his

Christmas service, to enjoy a meal well-imbued with a different type of Christmas spirit.

There was no extended Christmas holiday for the Excise men, who had to be alert to the possibilities of cargoes being unloaded at sheltered harbours, from where transport by packhorse through the mountains would ensure distribution in the valleys and towns of the Lakes area.

Ronald Gibbon was a Customs and Excise officer in Carlisle for twenty-four years. He spent the ten years of his retirement researching the documentary evidence of smuggling in Cumberland.

1745 began violently, 145 gallons of brandy and 8 of rum had been seized from Francis Blake, and two Customs men, Thomas Field and Thomas Inman had been detailed to arrest him. Near Whitehaven they were attacked by a group of men,

Harbour at Ravenglass with Black Combe in the background

whilst Blake and his family escaped into Scotland. 1745 was of course, the year of the Scottish Rising in support of Bonnie Prince Charlie. Revenue vessels were diverted to support the English army and navy. This gave an immediate boost to the smuggling trade.

Violence continued between the smugglers and the Excise men, with gang attacks resulting in a number of murders of Crown officials. But in spite of this, large quantities of contraband were seized and offered for sale.

A Customs Sale at Whitehaven in January of 1776 included:

2,097 gallons of brandy, 582 gallons of Geneva, 373 lbs Bohea tea and 56 lbs of raw coffee.

Subsequent sales were to include more exotic goods;

51 dozen stampt paper
11 pieces black binding
34 yards White Linen Cloth
93 lbs Prunes
132½ yards Flannel
44 Volumes Bound Books
5 hogsheads Turpentine
about 8 tons Tarred and White Cordage
69 lbs Glew
36 lbs Human Hair
16 dozen Pairs Women's Leather Gloves
2 pairs Cotton Stockings
14½ doz. Knives
36 doz. and 1 pair Buckles
11 bundles Fish Hooks
62 lbs Candles
3 lbs Hair Powder
288 lbs Raw Wool
270 casks Raisins of the Sun . . .

On Christmas Eve of 1784, the Customs Collector at Whitehaven was instructed to make a thorough search of the coast and inlets and to impound all 'illegal' boats. This referred to an Act which had been passed in the previous session of Parliament, which introduced a licensing system for boats; any vessels which were not duly licensed were liable to forfeiture. The Whitehaven Collector promptly seized two boats at Whitehaven, one at Workington and no less than twenty (the entire herring fleet) at Maryport. This action so incensed the lord of the manor that a formal protest was made to the Board of Customs in London. The Maryport boats were released except for any 'suspected or detected in any illicit practices' . . .

Many Cumbrians supported the smugglers against the Customs men. In December 1786 they had seized 11 ankers of brandy and a chest of tea from smugglers at Harrington, and were carrying it to Whitehaven when they were attacked near Moresby. The gang of eight men were beaten off, but only after 'a severe conflict'.

In January of 1819, a boat was seized at Harrington which had sailed over from the Isle of Man, included among its cargo were 1,000 packs of cards, for it must be remembered that card parties were very popular with Cumbrians over the Christmas period.

A French vessel, *de Vos* manned by a crew of about hundred and armed with twenty guns slipped considerable quantities of brandy, gin and tobacco ashore near Whitehaven in December 1820. Fortunately Excise officers seized much of it, including 1260 lbs of tobacco in the cart of a Common Carrier from Longtown. . . .

In January 1822 William Harding and four other men were apprehended carrying Scotch salt whilst crossing the new

bridge over the Esk. Harding, a shoemaker from Warwick Bridge, was carrying a three stone bag of salt, intending to kill, and salt down a pig, when two Customs men from Bowness, who had moored their boat below the bridge, ordered the men to halt. A scuffle ensued, and Harding was shot dead. The Coroner's jury found the officers guilty of murder, but they were acquitted at the Assizes two months later.

Whisky smuggling took place between England and Scotland. In January 1820, a number of persons from both sides of the Solway were in the habit of carrying whisky into Cumberland. For this purpose they used light tin containers, which were often shaped to fit the body. Fastened to the body by straps, these canisters which were known as 'Belly Cans' were almost undetectable when worn under a greatcoat.

The belly can held up to about two gallons, in addition, bladders were sometimes used in a similar way, or even more ingeniously fastened to the necks of dogs trained to swim across Border rivers.

An Excise Border Preventive Service established in 1830 gradually reduced the whisky smuggling. One man caught with two gallons of whisky was sentenced to 'the treadmill at Carlisle for three months'. . .

By 1855 excise duty on whisky was made the same for both Scotland and England, 'and the occupation of smuggler has become extinct; smuggling from the Isle of Man and elsewhere also declined'.

Nowadays, the greatest threat to the Customs and Excise officials during the days leading up to Christmas probably comes from the coachloads of Cumbrian housewives, returning from their assaults on the hypermarkets of Calais and Boulogne.

Weighed down with bottles of wine, burdened with brandy and liquers and festooned with garlands of garlic, they approach the blue suited Excise men at the Customs barricade.

Nervous, apprehensive, with feelings of guilt that need not be, they hurry through the Customs Hall waiting for the dreaded call; hoping to escape.

Huge relief as the one in front is stopped — nearly there — round the corner — out of sight of those piercing eyes. Made it — now for a quick slurp out of that half-finished bottle above the quota; the one we failed to finish on the boat.

The Aeroplane and Father Christmas

Today's children readily accept the thought of Father Christmas arriving by air from snow-covered Lapland. Some children actually become airborne themselves so that they can visit his toy workshops in the frozen north.

Sixty years ago, this was almost unthinkable. But the pilot of an aeroplane returning from an extraordinary trip, made it a memorable Christmas for a group of children in Windermere, as reported in the Westmorland Gazette, *of 24 December 1926.*

· A Lakes Christmas ·

Wednesday was the Christmas Treat day at the Ethel Hedley Crippled Children's Hospital, and was the most eventful day of the year for the little patients.

An unusual incident opened the proceedings – a forced descent by the Helvellyn bound airman, who had run short of petrol and after circling the head of Windermere Lake, effected a landing on Calgarth Park in full view of the crippled children. Here he remained for two hours and the excitement of the children was intense, especially as the event timed with the arrival of 'Father Christmas'.

> *Today one of the more surprising sights awaiting anyone who arrives at the summit of Helvellyn, Lakeland's third highest mountain at 3,118 feet, is a memorial stone commemorating another landing made by the same aircraft.*
>
> *The* Westmorland Gazette *carried a detailed account of the true purpose of the flight involved, the accomplishment of which is almost as unbelievable as the arrival of Father Christmas himself. . . .*

Mr J. Leeming, chairman of the Lancashire Aero Club, and Mr Bert Hinkler, the Manchester airman, succeeded in landing on Helvellyn on Wednesday . . .

. . . the arrival of the airmen on Helvellyn was witnessed by Mr E. Dodds, Professor of Greek at Birmingham University. The professor includes mountaineering among his hobbies and had taken advantage of a magnificent day to climb Helvellyn. It is understood that he is staying at Watermillock on the west side of Ullswater. There was no-one on the mountain by pre-arrangement but when the airmen discovered that Mr Dodds was on the summit when they landed, they secured from him the following certificate which they took back with them: 'I hereby certify that an aeroplane GEB.H pilots Bert

THE FIRST AEROPLANE TO
LAND ON A MOUNTAIN
IN GREAT BRITAIN
DID SO ON THIS SPOT
ON DECEMBER 22ND 1926
JOHN LEEMING AND
BERT HINKLER
IN AN AVRO 585 GOSPORT
LANDED HERE
AND AFTER A SHORT STAY
FLEW BACK TO WOODFORD

Commemorative stone on Helvellyn, the mountain on which
an aircraft landed

Hinkler and John Leeming – landed on the summit of
Helvellyn December 22nd 1926.' The scribbled document was
signed 'E.R. Dodds, Professor of Greek, Birmingham
University.'

The story of the flight.

The start of the hazardous adventure was made from Lancaster
in secret. Plans had been made some days previously for an
organised welcome on the mountain summit, including the
marking out of prepared landing places and the lighting of
fires to give the airman an indication of the direction and force
of the wind. On Wednesday however, there were no such
preparations and it was quite a coincidence that Mr Dodds was
climbing the mountain for his own recreation and had reached

the summit just about the time – 1.35 p.m. – when the aeroplane landed. The airmen's . . . in keeping their intentions secret was noted in case the weather should again prove unfavourable and the attempt once more fail. The machine used was an Avro-Gosport. Describing the trip to the Daily Despatch Mr Leeming said they started from Lancaster which had been their base since the beginning of the attempt, at 1 p.m. 'Hinkler and I', he said, 'were together in the plane which had behaved splendidly throughout. In a short time we had reached the Lake District and could see a wonderful panorama below. After passing Scafell, Helvellyn came into view. The visibility was quite good, although on occasions we ran into cloud banks.' The principal difficulty of the venture seems to have been the presence of bad air pockets in the neighbourhood of Helvellyn, and the airmen had a terrifying experience. 'In one gigantic air pocket,' said Mr Leeming, 'we fell five hundred feet like a stone. I had in my hand a letter to deliver to Mr Sandham the manager of the Thirlmere Waterworks. This was completely torn away. We have to be very thankful that we had our safety belts fastened or else we might both have been blown out of the plane time after time. On occasions while in the air pockets the machine was tossed about like a cork in the sea. The air pockets were the worst I have experienced and when we dropped five hundred feet, we seemed to be falling faster than gravity itself, as though some huge force was pressing us down. Bert Hinkler was lifted in the air, clear of his seat, and the cushion flew down, nobody knew where.'

Safe landing on the summit.
The landing on Helvellyn's summit was accomplished after circling three times in a descending spiral over the mountain, which was approached at a speed of eighty miles an hour. The aeroplane landed on the rough ground, and running over

stones, some of which were eighteen inches high, was stopped about thirty yards from the edge of the Striding Edge precipice, which is a sheer drop of 700 feet. Another danger immediately threatened the machine, just as the purpose of the flight had been achieved. When brought to a standstill, the machine had a tendency to roll backwards down the sloping summit. 'It was necessary', said Mr Leeming 'for Hinkler to keep the engine running at full power while I hurried out of the plane and placed stones under the wheels to keep it stationary.' Apparently the machine came to ground when flying northwards and ran a short distance up the steadily rising ground almost to the edge of the precipice. Describing the landing, Mr Leeming said, 'We made a splendid landing. Of course, we know every inch of the ground, but we did not land on either of the places selected. We had thought of landing some distance further away from th summit, but when we reached the mountain we decided to go out for it, and made the landing on a spot within ten yards of the heap of stones that marks the actual summit of the mountain. The landing itself was a much simpler affair than flying in the pockets we encountered on the way. There was never any danger from the precipice.'

When he landed, Mr Leeming approached Mr Dodds asking, 'Have you got a piece of paper sir?' Mr Dodds fumbled in his pockets and produced a bill for minor articles at the university. 'Never mind it will do,' said Mr Leeming, and Dodds then wrote the certificate of landing. Written in pencil in the cold atmosphere of the mountain top it was merely a scrawl, but it served its purpose. The airmen chatted with Mr Dodds for about twenty minutes and Mr Leeming took several photographs of Mr Hinkler in the areoplane.

'Took off over Striding Edge'
The intrepid airmen commenced their return journey by

taking off (according to the Manchester Guardian) over Striding Edge, about the point where it directly overlooks Red Tarn. The machine 'taxied' up the slope with difficulty, but gained flying speed just in time to see it safely off the edge of the precipice. The machine flew to Windermere, where the need for petrol forced to seek a landing. After circling several times round the head of Lake Windermere, with his engine missing badly, Mr Leeming made a successful landing in Calgarth Park . . . Mr Leeming made a successful flight from there to the Woodford aerodrome near Manchester which was reached about 4.30 p.m. just after darkness had fallen. Mr Leeming denied that the flight was undertaken as a 'stunt'. It was, he said, purely an effort to show that it is now possible for a modern aeroplane to land almost anywhere.

'It was certainly a very thrilling experience, particularly when we encountered the air pockets, for the "bumps" were really appalling, although it was quite calm down below, there was a keen wind when we descended from the plane on the moutain.' During the evening following his return to Manchester, Mr Leeming received innumerable congratulatory telegrams and telephone messages.

Flight watched from Grasmere.
The final stages of the flight were watched by many interested spectators in the neighbourhood of Grasmere and Wythburn, though no-one appears to have been able to follow the course of the machine to the actual point of landing. An aeroplane was seen over Wythburn at 1.45 p.m. It circled twice over Helvellyn's summit and then for a period of twenty minutes was lost to sight by those observing it. When it re-appeared, the aeroplane seemed to rise from the very top of the mountain and flew away in a southerly direction passing over Grasmere for the second time at 2.30 in the afternoon. Mr J. Sandham, who is employed on the Manchester Corporation's waterworks

at Thirlmere and to whom Mr Leeming was to have delivered a letter, saw the machine flying towards Helvellyn, but he was unable to follow it to the point at which the airmen alighted. He confirms the statements of other eye-witnesses that the machine was out of sight for about twenty minutes before it re-appeared and flew away southwards. In the evening, following Mr Leeming's arrival back at his base, Mr Tom Scott of the Rothay Hotel, Grasmere received a telephone message from him to the effect that he had accomplished his mission and had landed on the summit of Helvellyn and had flown away again. When the first news bulletin was broadcast from Manchester station on Wednesday evening, Mr Leeming briefly announced that he had successfully carried out his project and had landed on Helvellyn that afternoon. The announcement was received at the Rothay Hotel during dinner, and the company heartily applauded. Mr Leeming is the first aviator to effect a successful landing on a mountain summit.

View showing the southern approach to Helvellyn

38

from

Letters of William Wordsworth

ALAN G. GILL

Wordsworth admitted to being a reluctant letter writer, even in replying to his closest friends. Many of his letters begin with apologies for a lengthy delay in answering: 'When I look back on the length of time elapsed since my receipt of your last letter, I am overwhelmed with a sense of shame. . . .' A letter he wrote to Samuel Taylor Coleridge on Christmas Eve 1799 tells of how William and his sister Dorothy came to their new home of Dove Cottage just a few days before Christmas.

My dearest Coleridge,

We arrived here last Friday, and have now been four days in our new abode without writing to you, a long time, but we have been in such confusion as not to have had a moment's leisure . . .

D. is now sitting by me racked with the tooth-ache. This is a grievous misfortune as she has so much work for her needle among the bed curtains etc that she is absolutely buried in it. We have both caught troublesome colds in our new and almost empty house, but we hope to make it a comfortable dwelling. Our first two days were days of fear as one of the upstairs rooms smoked like a furnace, we have since learned that this is uninhabitable as a sitting room on this account; the other room however which is fortunately the one we intended for our *living* room promises uncommonly well; that is, the chimney draws perfectly and does not even smoke at the first lighting of the fire. In particular winds most likely we shall have *puffs of inconvenience*, but this I believe will be found a curable evil, by means of devils as they are called and other beneficent agents which we shall station at the top of the chimney if their services should be required. D. is much pleased with the house and *appurtenances* the orchard especially; in imagination she has already built a seat with a summer shed on the highest platform in this our little domestic slip of a mountain. The spot commands a view over the roof of our house, of the lake, the church, helm cragg, and two thirds of the vale . . .

The manners of the neighbouring cottagers have far exceeded our expectations . . . The people we have uniformly found kind-hearted frank and manly, prompt to serve without servility. This is but an experience of four days, but we have had dealings with persons of various occupations, and have had no reason whatever to complain.

We have agreed to give a woman who lives in one of the adjoining cottages two shillings a week for attending two or three hours a day to light fires wash dishes etc etc. In addition to this she is to have her victuals every Saturday when she will be employed in scouring, and to have her victuals likewise on other days if we should have visitors and she is wanted more than usual. We could have had this attendance for eighteen pence a week but we added the sixpence for the sake of the poor woman who is made happy by it. The weather since our arrival has been a keen frost, one morning two thirds of the lake were covered with ice which continued all the day but to our great surprize the next morning, though there was no intermission of the frost had entirely disappeared. The ice had been so thin that the wind had broken it up, and most likely driven it to the outlet of the lake. Rydale is covered with ice, clear as polished steel, I have procured a pair of skates and tomorrow mean to give my body to the wind, – not however without reasonable caution . . . Composition I find invariably pernicious to me, and even penmanship if continued for any length of time at one sitting. I shall therefore wish you goodnight my beloved friend, a wish, with a thousand others, in which D. joins me. I am afraid half of what I have written is illegible, farewell . . .

> *The letter continues on 27 December with a description of how the Wordsworths travelled by coach and on foot from Yorkshire into what was then the county of Westmorland. After leaving Askrigg they visited Hardraw falls. His account gives an insight as to their remarkable ability as walkers.*

. . . and will you believe me when I tell you that we walked the next ten miles, by the watch over a high moutain road, thanks to the wind that drove behind us and the good road, in two hours and a quarter, a marvellous feat of which D. will long to tell. Well! we rested in a tempting inn, close by Garsdale chapel, a lowly house of prayer in a charming little valley, here we stopped a quarter of an hour and then off to Sedbergh 7 miles further in an hour and thirty five minutes, the wind was still at our backs and the road delightful. I must hurry on, next morning we walked to Kendal, 11 miles, a terrible up and down road, in 3 hours, and after buying and ordering furniture, the next day by half past four we reached Grasmere in a post chaise. So ends my long story. God bless you,

W.W.

from

Confessions of an Opium Eater

THOMAS DE QUINCEY

Thomas de Quincey moved into Dove Cottage, the former home of William Wordsworth, in 1809. He was a great admirer of Wordsworth, and their friendship developed through correspondence while de Quincey was still a student at Oxford.

In later years, the friendship came under strain through de Quincey's addiction to opium. In a letter of 1826 to a publisher who wanted de Quincey as a contributor, William Wordsworth warned, 'do not be tempted to depend on him. He is strangely irresolute'. The following extracts describe Thomas de Quincey's happiness at winter evenings spent at Dove Cottage, Grasmere.

And therefore I will lay down an analysis of happiness; . . .
Let there be a cottage, standing in a valley, . . .
Let it, however, not be spring, nor summer, nor autumn; but winter in its sternest shape. This is a most important point in the science of happiness. And I am surprised to see people overlook it, as if it were actually matter of congratulation that

winter is going, or, if coming, is not likely to be a severe one. On the contrary, I put up a petition, annually, for as much snow, hail, frost, or storm of one kind or another, as the skies can possibly afford. Surely everybody is aware of the divine pleasures which attend a winter fireside – candles at four o'clock, warm hearth-rugs, tea, a fair tea-maker, shutters closed, curtains flowing in ample draperies on the floor, whilst the wind and rain are raging audibly without, . . .

All these are items in the description of a winter evening which must surely be familiar to everybody born in a high latitude. And it is evident that most of these delicacies cannot be ripened, without weather stormy or inclement in some way or other. I am not particular whether it be snow, or black frost, or wind so strong that (as Mr Anti-slavery Clarkson says) 'you may lean your back against it like a post'. . .

 . . . I cannot relish a winter night fully, if it be much past St. Thomas's Day, and have degenerated into disgusting tendencies towards vernal indications: in fact, it must be divided by a thick wall of dark nights from all return of light and sunshine. Start, therefore, at the first week of November: thence to the end of January, Christmas Eve being the meridian line, you may compute the period when happiness is in season, which in my judgement enters the room with the tea-tray. For tea . . . will always be the favourite beverage of the intellectual . . .

But here, to save myself the trouble of too much verbal description, I will introduce a painter, and give him directions for the rest of the picture . . .

Paint me, then, a room seventeen feet by twelve, and not more than seven and a half feet high . . . Make it populous with books; and, furthermore, paint me a good fire; and furniture plain and modest, befitting the unpretending cottage of a scholar. And near the fire paint me a tea-table; and (as it is clear that no creature can come and see one on such a stormy night) place only two cups and saucers on the tea-tray; . . . And, as it is very unpleasant to make tea, or to pour it out for one's-self, paint me a lovely young woman sitting at the table . . .

Pass, then, my good painter, to something more with its power; and the next article brought forward should naturally be myself – a picture of the Opium-eater, with his 'little golden receptacle of the pernicious drug' lying beside him on the table . . .

I admit that, naturally, I ought to occupy the foreground of the picture; that being the hero of the piece, or (if you choose) the criminal at the bar, my body should be had into court . . .

. . . up to the middle of (1817) I judge myself to have been a happy man; and the elements of that happiness I have endeavoured to place before you, in the sketch of the interior of a scholar's library, in a cottage among the mountains, on a stormy winter evening, rain driving vindictively and with malice aforethought against my windows, and darkness such that you cannot see your own hand when held up against the sky.

Party Time at Sawrey

In some Cumbrian villages during the 1920s, a tradition developed for the local 'gentry' to provide Christmas parties for the village children.

Hill Top, Sawrey, the former home of Beatrix Potter, is closed and shuttered for the winter

Sawrey, near Hawkshead, was one such area, where the children looked forward with great excitement to the parties that were held during the two weeks of the school holidays. Many wealthy people made their homes in the large houses that sprang up round the twin villages of Far Sawrey and Near Sawrey, for they were within easy reach of industrialized Lancashire – a forerunner of the modern commuter belt. Besides this, it had also become fashionable to spend time, or live 'at the lakes'. One notable inhabitant of Sawrey was Beatrix Potter, the prolific writer of children's books. In October of 1913 she married William Heelis and finally settled in the village which she had come to know and love through spending many holidays in the area.

Thus, in the 1920s, it was as Mrs Heelis, farmer and wife of a country solicitor, that she was known to the village people.

On at least three occasions, she gave a party at Christmas for the children.

Notable she may have been, but her parties did not create a lasting impression in the mind of a young girl who attended those parties. Now many years later, and in her seventies, that young girl was persuaded to recall memories of the parties she attended when living at Sawrey.

For her, the best parties of all were those given by Mr Edmondson, a colliery owner who with his family lived in the large house of 'Briarswood'. Mr Edmondson was a person of some standing for he employed a number of servants, among which were two chauffeurs. 'Mr Edmondson gave grand parties. There was always a huge Christmas tree in the hall of his house, and there were all sorts of wonderful things to eat; jellies, trifles, cakes, all the things that children like.'

Every child in the village received an invitation to Mr Edmondson's party, even the babies. 'There would be a good number of us there, for everyone had a large family in those days.' The party was held in the ballroom of his house, which was a very grand place. Mr Edmondson and his family organized the party themselves, and after tea, 'Mr Edmondson would show us a Charlie Chaplin film, now that was really something in those days'.

Everyone came away from Mr Edmondson's party clutching a really beautiful present, such as a doll, or for the boys there would be something like a fishing rod, or a football.

By comparison, the parties that Mrs Heelis gave were 'very frugal affairs'. They were held in a barn adjoining one of her farms, and although it was swept clean, it was a chilly place to hold a party. There was no recollection of grand things to eat at those parties, jam sandwiches was the only food that came to mind; and there was no memory of bringing anything home, other than an orange; thoughts recalled from the discriminating memory of an eleven year old. Although Mrs Heelis attended the

parties, she made no attempt to join in, or help organize the games, but would sit in the background watching the goings on, while the festivity was left in the hands of Miss Choyce, a friend of Mrs Heelis. The villagers regarded Miss Choyce as a sort of companion, who would often come and stay with her.

Only the older children of the village were invited to these parties and after tea, they played games. It was as a result of one of these games that the parties given by Mrs Heelis came to an end. One little boy, called Henry, insisted on untying all the bows of the girls' pinafores and hair ribbons, much to the annoyance of Mrs Heelis.

The following year, when the invitations were sent out, Henry's mother was told that he could only attend the party if he promised to be on his best behaviour. This so annoyed Henry's mother, that she refused to let not only Henry, but the rest of her children, go to the party, and there was no further memory of any more parties given by Mrs Heelis.

The children of Sawrey were not really aware that Mrs Heelis was any more remarkable than the rest of the 'gentry' that lived in and around the village. They were rather frightened of her, and kept well away from her orchards, although one lad was bold enough to steal some of her apples, by creeping through a gap in a hedge. The theft was discovered, and a repetition prevented by the planting of a prickly holly bush in the gap.

They knew that she wrote books, for *The Tale of Pigling Bland*, published 1913, featured a great friend of the village children. That was Mr Fleming, the local carter, who would give the children lifts when he saw them walking along the roads, and to see a picture of 'their cart' in a book, was a great thrill. Mr Fleming was remembered as 'a grand old chap who gave us presents at Christmas, one of which was *The Tale of Pigling Bland*'.

As well as the parties given by the 'gentry', there was always

Part of the village of Near Sawrey, from the hill overlooking
Hill Top Farm

the 'Village Party' to look forward to. This was a grand affair
and went on for three days. In the days leading up to
Christmas, food and money was collected from every household in the village. The large houses were very generous with
their donations, and when the time for the party came, tables
were loaded with sandwiches and pies, cakes and sweets, jellies
and trifles as well as all kinds of fruit and nuts.

The first of the three days was the day of the children's party
when a hearty tea was followed by games played in an
atmosphere of noisy excitement.

The second day was the turn of the grown-ups to enjoy
themselves, but the children were also involved, for after the
adults had eaten, the children had to provide the entertainment. 'Each child had to learn a piece, recite a poem, sing
a song, or perform a dance.'

NOW TO BUSINESS.

The CHRISTMAS SHOW this year will be the best on Record. You will see one of the Finest Sights ever witnessed in Bowness as regards Fancy Drapery and Toys, &c., &c.

The Old Man is bringing a Bigger Load than ever.

Presents to suit all ages, fra a Penny upbank.

Such as Lions, Tigers, Rocking Horses, Wolves, Spotted Leopards Monkeys, Elephants, Hedghogs, and Bears, Hungry Harry, Taleless Donkeys, Cungering Tricks, Clowns, Table Tennis, Tools, John Gilpin, Pop Guns, Baloons, Shows, Paint Boxes, Furniture, Farm Yards, Railways, Noah's Arks, Crocodiles, Hagworms, Gorillas, Moudywarps, and Baa Lambs, Ullets, Jerusalem Poneys and Donks, White Mice, Hindy Rubber Men and Wimmen, Bom-boms and Watterhasks, and o macks a Musical Instruments to hoful to partickelarise, Rynosscrusses, Mountebank Fellas, Motor Cars, Football Games, Motor Car Races, Mint Lozengers, Worm Powders, Dolly Tubs, Spectickels, Mice Traps, Teeth Combs, Picture Books, Snakes up Ladders, Treeakle Toffee, China Tea Sets, Trumpets, Guns, Swords, Cork Soles, Folse Teeth, and Games be t' hunderd ev o descriptions, &c., &c. But ya mun cum en see fer yersels.

BUY EARLY.

ADMISSION FREE. Children Half-price.

CLOTHING CLUB.

Don't fergit ta tell ya nebbers an relations, an yersels as weel, thet wen t' Cards cum oot, if ivver they dew again e this wurld, ta spend em 't Fent Shop, ye'l git yer munney's worth, en a Present as usual.

Registry Office for Servants.

Ladies! If you want to catch a Good Servant, set your Trap in our Office and Bait it with a Shilling.

The Oldest Registry Office in the Lake District.

FRANK ROBINSON, Draper, WINDERMERE.

Advert for Frank Robinson's Christmas Show in Windermere, 1906

49

Whatever the choice, it had been thoroughly learned, and feverishly rehearsed in the weeks leading up to Christmas so that it would be perfect on the night. The third day was the day of the Whist Drive and Dance. Prizes for the Whist Drive came from donations given during the 'great collection'.

The dance brought the party to a close with everyone joining in the fun, and the music provided by a local band. 'They were grand parties,' the seventy-year-old recalled. 'They don't have parties like that any more.'

from

Tom Rumney of Mellfell

A.W. RUMNEY

Tom Rumney was a Cumbrian statesman, the local term for a yeoman farmer. He was born in 1764, the second son of William and Mary Rumney of Mellfell, a farm at the foot of Little Mell Fell near Ullswater.

After his father died, his parson uncle took over the responsibility for placing Thomas in work with a West Indian merchants office in London. He returned to Mellfell

House when he inherited the estate on the death of his eldest brother.

Thomas Rumney was a prolific letter writer and diarist. His great-great-nephew A.W. Rumney compiled the book Tom Rumney of Mellfell, *published in 1936, from these writings. It includes extracts from a diary of 1805, in which there are entries for every day in December except the 30th.*

1st – The weather excessively wet and stormy. Paid Thomas Gasgarth his expenses in finding my two Scots (cattle) strayed off Uldale – 8s. 6d.

3rd – Sent four loads of oats to mill per William Clark who brought a load of lime home. I painted a coop cart brown.

4th – Mr John Rowe brought us 1½ doz. of charr and ½ doz.

Ullswater from Pooley Bridge from an engraving by Allan & Pickering *c.* 1830

trout. Joe Harrison sawing up the large oak tree at Mellfell, which was very difficult to get upon the horse.

6th – John Thompson son of Lowthwaite ran away last night and was found this morning at Dalemain, his mother having beat him.

8th – Put up railings for my Scotch cattle to eat straw out of. Had the produce of $2\frac{1}{2}$ loads of oats for family use.

10th – Began to quarry for stones to fill drains in Brown High Field.

13th – The most thunder I ever heard at this season, much rain and hail and the wind excessively high. Geo. Martin bought a cow called Mary off Jos Todd for near £20.

16th – Went to Penrith. Forwarded to the Rev Mr Richardson a 1lb pot of fresh charr per mail coach from the New Crown Inn. Paid carriage to Manchester 2s. 2d. Bought a Spokeshave for 1s. 9d.

20th – Last night very stormy with tremendous high winds and rain. My Tongue pond overflowed on every side and part of front washed down. I waded up to mid-leg in cutting the running wider and was obliged to change even my shirt after being so drenched with rain.

22nd – Spoke to the maid servant in serving the pigs in a wasteful manner. Jos Todd's dog, Boy killed a weasel in the Acres. I a second time hunted it the forenoon.

25th – Christmas Day. At breakfast the servants as were present had the Collect read and family morning prayers. The day stormy with wind.

29th – Carted straw to Back Highs. Wm. Clarke thrashed barley. Jos Todd bled my Scotch calf. Have caught a most violent cold.

31st – Had a very bad night with my cold. Sent one load of oats and a bushel of barley to the mill for the hogs. Paid John Wilkinson for catching moles last year for two tenements at 1s–2s.

A final entry from his accounts of 2 December 1835 reads;
Gave a treat at the Beacon Hill upon Mell Fell upon the staking out of my allotment comprising the Mountain chiefly consisting of about 154 acres. Almost 50 people partook of rum and milk, 19 bottles of spirits was consumed much mirth took place. The day was favourable with much jollification. We will say farewell to Tom Rumney of Mellfell.

Christmas on the La'al Ratty

IAN AND GILLIAN STANISTREET

Gillian and Ian Stanistreet brought their three children from their home in Johannesburg, South Africa, to spend Christmas 1990 in England with their families.

One of the highlights of the trip was taking the children on the La'al Ratty to meet Father Christmas.

The La'al Ratty is a miniature railway, owned and managed by the Ravenglass and Eskdale Railway Company Limited. It was originally built to carry ore from the Eskdale mines in the nineteenth century. It had an erratic industrial life before being bought by public subscription in 1960 for the express purpose of saving the line.

The company, assisted by volunteers from the Raven-

'The Devon' — one of the engines on the 3 ft guage railway

glass and Eskdale Railway Preservation Society, now run the railway for the benefit of visitors. The La'al Ratty is one of Lakeland's best loved tourist attractions. Each Christmas time, special trains take family parties the seven mile journey, through some of Lakeland's finest scenery, to meet Father Christmas. The name T'la'al Ratty trips off everyone's tongue, without being fully understood. La'al is Cumbrian for 'little' and 'ratty' refers either to the derivation from the contractor's name of Ratcliffe, or the affectionate term the old miners used to refer to the line as 'the la'al rat track'. The choice is yours.

We woke on Saturday morning to see snow flurries swirling past the window. The world outside was white, an added bonus for the day when we, visitors from Africa, were due to

Logo of the 'Ratty Christmas Special'

55

go on a very special train ride to meet a very special person. On the other hand, we wondered, would we get through to the station? Would the train still be running?

Out of bed early, quickly ready and into the cars. Baby Claire, with still bleary eyes, having no idea of what the day would bring, sat in the back of our car between brothers Robert seven, and Kevin five. Their grandparents took nine-year-old Rebecca from next door in their car. Would we get through in conditions which had cut into the heart of the Lake District, seemingly, straight from Siberia?

Away from Great Clifton, past Harrington and Whitehaven – we were through. The comparative warmth of the Irish Sea had kept the coastal roads clear of snow and ice. Ravenglass Station greeted us with snowball-fresh snow and canned carols on the tannoy. There was barely time to buy emergency rations of chocolate and postcards to send to folks back home in Africa before boarding the little carriages.

'At least they are heated,' we said to the man who kept the shop.

'If you're lucky,' he growled back.

But who cared. We were all double-socked, buttoned and hooded, the train was running, we were going to meet a celebrity. Boot village or bust.

Grandmas and grandas, mummies and daddies, boys, girls and babies all converge on the narrow little carriages. It is staggering to think we can travel on a 15-inch gauge track without tipping over. No time to look at the engine yet, that will have to wait. A slight shudder and we are off, rolling slowly across the bridge over the road before gradually gathering speed.

This is the way to travel. The smell and taste of coal smoke bringing back memories of train rides long ago. After passing Muncaster Mill, the track climbs into the Cumbrian foothills.

We pass fields of sheep, all facing the same way but huddled into the lee of a drystone wall. Further, the snow becomes thicker and the sheep look a little more miserable. We pass small stations, no stopping today. Who in their right mind would travel on the little train on a cold winter's day? We would – we're on our way to meet somebody important.

On we go into the white woodland, to a section of double track where the uptrain can pass the downtrain. We stop. No, it's not a station. Maybe the engine has broken down? No, it's not that either. Then the reason becomes apparent.

He's arrived; it's him; it's FATHER CHRISTMAS. Here he comes, his sleigh pulled down the other track hitched to a small, green engine, normally called the River Irt, but today renamed Rudolph in honour of the occasion.

Boys and girls scramble out of the train to meet him, despite parents' best efforts to hold them back; then, swept up

Arrival of Father Christmas at Dalegarth station

57

in the excitement, they too get out to record the scene on film. 'Hello everybody, Merry Christmas. Let's all get into the train,' Father Christmas says as he walks towards the rear coach carrying his big sack.

The train moves on. Of course, who else would ENJOY being in the middle of a wood, in the snow, on a winter's day in Cumbria? It's nothing to Father Christmas; he lives at the North Pole you know. . . .

The train stops again, and Father Christmas gets into OUR coach.

'Hello Father Christmas.'

'And what do you want me to bring you?'

'A computer please,' said Rebecca.

'To help you with your sums?'

'A space gun,' says Robert.

'And I want a space gun,' says Kevin.

'Not to shoot your Daddy, I hope? And what does Claire want?'

Nobody knows. 'I'll just bring her a nice surprise,' says Father Christmas.

The train stops again and off he goes to the next coach. How DOES he remember all those toys, for all those children?

We arrive at the end of the line. Dalegarth Station at Boot must have one of the prettiest settings of anywhere, especially when everything is white. Scafell to the north looks like a Christmas pudding and high snow-covered crags fill the views in all other directions.

The passengers follow Father Christmas into the station. There's mince pies and orange juice for the children, and mince pies and something stronger for the grown-ups. Father Christmas sits on a throne of Christmas presents. Children gather round, hanging on to his every word and movement.

'Joe Straughton,' Father Christmas shouts.

A small boy is taken up to receive his present.

'Jane Kendall.'

Another excited face moves up to the throne.

'Claire Stanistreet.'

There's big excitement as she is carried to receive her present, and Mummy follows many others in recording the event on film.

Robert's face drops. 'I'm eldest, why aren't I first?' he seems to be asking himself.

'Patricia Lee.'

A long list of names follows, Robert's face looks concerned.

'Kevin Stanistreet.'

Kevin has to be directed through the now developed crush of children, past a worried Robert, to pick up his parcel.

'Kelly Sewell.'

'Rebecca Wilson.'

Robert looks frantic as more names follow.

'Robert Stanistreet.'

Relief and excitement floods over his face as he picks up his present, almost forgetting to say 'Thank you.'

There is a JCB digger for Robert, a tractor set for Kevin, a shape sorter bus for Claire and a colouring set for Rebecca. Hands and minds are occupied for a few minutes before it's back to the platform to have a look at the little red engine called River Mite which had hauled us to Dalegarth, and Kevin is allowed to sit in the little cab.

'As long as he doesn't touch anything', says the driver.

A runaway train is the last thing he needs on a day like this.

There is certainly much to attract small fingers; levers, dials pipes and taps, all made of gleaming brass, glow in the light of the engine's small fire.

Now it's time to return to our seats on the train. Father Christmas gets into a carriage he hasn't visited yet, the crowd sorts itself out, and we are off, back down the track. A few stops on the way to allow Father Christmas to visit the few

The 'Santa Special', ready to return to Ravenglass

remaining carriages and then we're back at his sleigh. 'Bye bye Father Christmas', as he waves his way to his return up the track.

The little train, full of happy children, resumes its return journey to Ravenglass. Did one of the daddies REALLY see some of Father Christmas' reindeer grazing away in the field near where he met us? All the children are awarded two railway engine badges, like medals for a mission safely accomplished.

The train chugged into Ravenglass station.

'Well Robert, did you remember to tell Father Christmas that he must bring your presents to Cumbria this year, and not to Africa?'

'Ah, but Daddy, it wasn't the REAL Father Christmas.'

'Why on earth do you say that?'

'Because when I looked I saw the piece of elastic behind his head, holding on his beard.'

At the station, we at last had time for a snowball fight before grandma's sumptuous picnic revived cold fingers and toes. Four very happy children were loaded into the cars for a sleepy return journey. As far as they were concerned, they might just as well have been travelling back in Father Christmas' sleigh.

A Winter Ascent of Skiddaw

Frances Wilson, the BBC breakfast time weather forecaster promised a fine day; indeed a glorious day, he said. Just the day, I decided, to climb Skiddaw.

My route was up the well worn tourist track that rises high above Keswick, but progress was slow as the superb lighting effects, rippling round the fells that enclosed Derwentwater, called for many photographic stops.

Heavy, black cloud hung over Borrowdale and Newlands, torn apart by shafts of light from the sun, edging the blackness with a silvered raggy rim. The light played across the valley fields, giving a patterning effect of vivid green, the brilliance fading as shadow chased the sun.

As height was gained, snow lay underfoot – a scattering only at first, then gradually spreading and deepening till the stony path was hidden. Patterns of many boot marks indicated the steady procession there had been the previous day. Deeper snow lay ahead. Fresh fallen, it had covered the footprints so evident at the lower heights. The track to the summit, so broad and clear in fine weather, bore now only my single line of footprints.

Over Great Calva and Knott, there was heavy cloud, black-based cumulus mushrooming up. The wind was strong and cold. At the col between Skiddaw and its Little Man, it scythed through, penetrating with its sharpness, whipping up

the loose snow to sting the face and stream the hair. Deep snow covered the shaly slopes, exhilarating to climb it in steps knee deep, but firm underfoot.

I climbed on, up to the bared grey shale, where the wind had seared the snow away; each stone ice rimed and crusted in the gaps. The wind was stronger, driving feeling from ears and nose, numbing fingers and drawing frozen tears from watering eyes.

Underfoot, the ice-glazed stones of the summit plateau needed a careful step as the wind battered with force as I intruded on its private world.

The stone shelters of the summit belied their name, for they were filled to the brim with crisp, hard, snow. The edges of the shelter stones wore snow-feathering streamers, shaped by the wind and frozen into formation like the plumage of some snow bird. They fused together, preened by forces of chilly power, and gleamed with a blued sparkle as the sunlight tipped their trails.

I used my ice axe to hack away the snow from inside the shelter, warmed by the exertion to gain a brief respite from the wind. Over the rim of the shelter stones could be seen High Spy, Dale Head Hindscarth and others, their summits of white contrasting with the deep blue sky.

This was no place to linger with the wind biting and snapping round my improvised shelter. Time to head back, leaning into the wind.

There was silvered light on Derwentwater as it caught the sun's rays. The green fields far below seemed at odds with my barren and hostile landscape; only a short distance away, but seasons apart in mood and weather.

I hurried down the snow slope – heels in – grip – jump – with a childlike enjoyment of the unsullied snow, alone in an icy landscape where mine were the only steps.

Out of the wind at last behind the slopes of Little Man, there was time to head across to Lonscales Fell. Gone was the

Brief sunlight on Derwentwater seen through snow clouds
on Skiddaw

usual boggy ground, the only yielding surface was clean and white. I followed a fence up to an apology of a cairn which was only a rusty fence post surrounded by a few lumps of slate. The surrounding area was clear of snow where the drab grass of winter showed through.

I retraced my steps to pick up the line of a minor track that joined the main path near a stile. The snow was left behind with the wind, as the shoulder of the mountain created its own shelter.

The stile is an easy place to gaze down over the Vale of Keswick, with wood worn smooth by many hands, slippery to the touch. The lake below was crinkled and wrinkled like a crumpled sheet of tinfoil opened out. Light glanced off in brilliant patches and the black islands stood out in relief. There was more brilliance as the sun illuminated the snow on Sail and Eel Crags, before sliding along to pick out Grisedale.

64

The lesser heights of Catbells and Barrow looked almost naked, denied the mantle of dignity sported by the higher tops. Beyond, Bowfell, Great End and Gable frowned down, no sun had kissed their tops today. The depth of cloud lay heavy on their summits. The wood of the stile was smooth and warm to the touch, a quiet place to watch and admire the changing kaleidoscope of pattern and colour in the valley below.

Christmas in Company

EVELYN ADAMS MBE

In cities and towns throughout the country, Christmas means a time of intensified loneliness for some people. No partner, no family, no friend even to share the long hours of a Christmas Day. What to most people is a happy time, is for them, just another day. Cumbrian towns are no different to any others, for they too have their share of lonely people. But there are those who are prepared to share their Christmas, to make Christmas Day a day to remember, for those who would otherwise have preferred to forget.

Evelyn Adams is one of those caring people, and her story tells of how she took on the responsibility of creating, with others, a joyous day for thirty elderly and lonely people; a day when they spent 'Christmas in Company'.

· *A Lakes Christmas* ·

Why shouldn't Workington have what Whitehaven had? For three-quarters of 1990 the thought occupied all spare moments of my mind, until finally action was decided upon. What was this mysterious and desirable something that Whitehaven had, that Workington had not? It was a get-together of elderly people who would otherwise have spent Christmas alone. In 1989, I had helped with organizing Christmas activities in that town for just such a group.

A great desire that something similar should happen in Workington took hold of me. However, it may well have remained only a desire had a friend not expressed similar hopes, and more to the point backed them up with the promise of a donation of fifty pounds from a group willing to give to a worthy cause.

The message was loud and clear – DO SOMETHING ABOUT THIS – but how? Question – short of knocking on doors and asking the occupiers personal questions about how they were going to spend Christmas Day, how does one find people that are likely to be on their own? Second question – where could I find others to help me care for these people, should I actually be able to find any? Answer – contact the caring organizations, social services, and the Council of Churches to see if they could suggest anyone. I set about doing this in September and there followed a time of waiting while committees met and individuals thought. Also I may add, prayers ascended, that somehow if guests were forthcoming, cars and drivers, potato peelers and carrot slicers, washers up etc. might also materialize.

Then the responses began to come in. First, a venue, a purpose designed building ideal for our guests. It was heated, decorated for the festive day, a good kitchen, toilets for both handicapped and able-bodied, and plenty of parking within easy reach. It was ours for the day.

Volunteers offered to spend a full or part day to help look

after the guests. Money donations, large and small began to roll in. A really terrific offer of help came in the form of not one, but two buses equipped with lifts for wheelchairs and zimmer users; plus offers of help from two volunteer bus drivers. There were also offers of help from volunteers with their own private vehicles. Transport worries were now non-existent. Promises of food for Christmas Day came in daily. Mince pies to the right; sausage rolls to the left; trifles and scones; sandwiches and chocolate cake.

'Could I make some gingerbread?' from a friend.

'I'll be making you some fresh mince pies on Christmas Eve,' from another. With tactful thanks, I suggested a diversion to 'fairy cakes'. Some little Christmas cakes were offered by another friend, an ex-domestic science teacher. Food aplenty seemed to be available, but looming in the back of my mind, like a storm cloud on Garden Party day, was the thought of mountains of potatoes, carrots and Brussels sprouts to wash, peel and chop. Then, reading through the local free newspaper, I saw the answer – 'Redi-Veg'.

'Leave it to us,' they said . . . . I did. Sure enough, bags of beautifully prepared vegetables arrived on Christmas Eve.

Early on, in the planning stages, ready-cooked turkey slices from a local shop was to be the basis of the Christmas dinner. These plans were abandoned when the offer of chickens was made known to me. I quickly followed up the offer to ascertain whether the said chickens would be alive, dead, feathered, plucked, frozen, or hopefully, cooked. More to the point, how many? 'How many do you want?' I was asked. 'Enough to feed 36,' I replied.

They would be minus feathers, and innards, but raw. Thought would have to be given to their preparation for the table, but something might turn up: and it did, or rather, SHE did. While wandering through town in early December, my mind far removed from the problem of raw chickens, I was

stopped by one of the volunteer drivers. He introduced his wife to me. She proceeded to ask a question which was music to my ears. 'Could I come and cook for you on Christmas Day?'

She had been a professional cook and was used to catering for large numbers. Talk about being welcomed with open arms. Needless to say, the cook, the vegetables and the chickens were united with very satisfactory results on the DAY.

A lady in the Social Services Department had prepared attractive invitations to send out to potential guests, which among other things included two little words 'and entertainment'. At that time, ideas of entertainment were a matter of hope and faith, rather than actual fact. However, over the weeks leading up to the 25th, first a magician, then folk singers and guitarists offered to give their time, to share Christmas with us. It was all beginning to come together. I distinctly felt like an elderly Anneka Rice, facing up to a challenge.

December 25th proved to be a wonderfully memorable day. The volunteer transport brought in our guests to the welcome of a hot cup of tea or coffee which helped them to relax as all were introduced to each other. With some, introductions were unnecessary as they renewed friendships from long ago.

They joined in the choruses of folk songs, or clapped their hands and tapped their feet as the day made a lively start. The mayor and his family came to see us, not a formal duty as part of his civic round, but an extension of friendship which was really appreciated.

Then came the Christmas dinner; we sat in groups at small tables within easy chatting range of each other for friendly contact. We were of many creeds, or none, but all joined in a prayer of thanks for so much giving and sharing that had made the day possible.

Crackers were pulled, party hats worn to attack the fruit salad, chicken, bacon, sausage, stuffing and all those vegetables. Somehow the trifle and rum butter, mints, apple juice,

tea and coffee was squeezed down before we all staggered away from our tables to relax with some informal carol singing and the old time songs.

We shared the gravity of the Queen's speech, and then forgot the world's problems as our magician entertained and bewildered us. Then it was time for tea. What – more food . . .

So generous had the townsfolk been with money and gifts, there were presents for everyone, and boxes of goodies to take home to enjoy on Boxing Day.

Every single person, guest or helper, enjoyed the day. The helpers felt the true joy of giving, while the guests had the unfamiliar feeling of being wanted. Throughout the day, photographs were taken to record the smiles, the new friendships forged, the old revived; the pleasures experienced but above all, the blessing received from spending time together as one big happy family. Workington did have what Whitehaven had, and hopefully will continue to have in years to come, 'Christmas in Company'.

"Don't Drink and Drive"

It may come as a surprise to many people that the drunken driver is not a modern day problem. As long ago as 1898, there were requests not to ply coach or cab drivers with 'drink'. One such request appeared in the Whitehaven News *of 22nd December 1898.*

Sir,

It may not be generally known that the Post-Master General yearly issues a circulation to all householders earnestly requesting them not to offer intoxicants to the postmen at Christmas. The B.W.T.A. invite the attention of householders to the danger in which others may be placed through their intended kindness during the approaching season. Postmen, cabmen and messengers will naturally receive Christmas hospitality. The question is, what form shall it take? If a glass of beer or spirits is given to the man at the door, it may be one of many given to him that day and he may return home intoxicated, or injured through the drink, may even lose his place, a result the giver never intended. We all know as a matter of fact that there are among the class referred to, men, to whom the offer of a single glass is a cruel temptation to men whose former lives have been blighted by drink, and who are now fighting bravely against yielding to their former besetment. Therefore let a cup of good coffee, or tea, or cocoa be prepared beforehand to offer with the usual 'Christmas Box' to those whose services at this season help largely towards the making for us all 'A Merry Christmas',

Yours truly

H. Jackson Palmer.

from

Wanderings in Lakeland

WILLIAM T. PALMER

William T. Palmer was born at Burneside, Kendal. He wrote many books on his native Lakeland, drawing on experiences gained as he wandered about the fells and dales, lakes and rivers and moors. He studied the people with whom he came into contact – farmers, shepherds, coachmen, huntsmen and all manner of country folk. He came of country stock, for his father was once a drover, and his grandfather a shepherd. Rambler, cyclist, ornithologist, naturalist, geographer are all facets which add authority to his writing, which tells us what the Lake District was like before the invasion of motor transport.

71

· A Lakes Christmas ·

Coach and four on Dunmail Raise, 1841

The Christmas Mail

The drivers who brought Christmas to Ambleside and Grasmere wore the vermilion jackets of the 'Royal Mail', and their
four horses had a rare load of folks returning for the holiday at
home, for scrambles among the rocks and ridges, as well as
bringing our precious missives.

At Christmas time, the whisky flowed like water round the
postman who brought up the mail, be the day frosty or dirty or
merely unpleasant. One has known the Christmas mail come
through the pass on a day of raging snow, with drifts among
the wheels, extra horses and a postillion on the leaders. It was
such a morning that old Jim alluded to when we were driving
through the dark morning to Grasmere. 'They tells me that
motors are going to be put on this job; but believe me, it can't
be done. Them hosses can either see, or hear, or smell their

way in the worst storm as ever blew, and they never swerve a
foot from their place on the road.'

Many a Christmas mail had old Jim brought to the village,
and the way his mail slipped about the ice-bound roads was
something to remember. In these days racing motor-cyclists
dash about dirt tracks and skid their corners; wonders never
cease, but old Jim and other drivers of the Christmas mails half
a century ago did the same thing, and a plunging horse-team
and a hummocky roads added sensation. To me old Jim, who
drove until the last horsemail in Westmorland was swept away
by the motor van, was a link with the great coach drivers of the
past.

Royalty, nobles and the rich had their private coaches, even
in Queen Elizabeth's time, but the public service which
gradually built up Christmas on the road did not begin until
much later.

It is stated that pedlars and packmen walked alongside the
travelling coaches and offered their wares. What an opportunity for a Christmas bazaar. In 1754 a Manchester firm
'undertook' that their conveyance would reach London in four
and a half days.

It was not until 1784 that the Christmas mail, such as it
was, went by coach instead of post boys and mounted couriers.
The mails must start prompt and run to the minute, summer
and winter alike. And a coachman who received his mails late
was expected to make up lost time on his stage. The Glasgow
– Carlisle coach averaged $11\frac{1}{2}$ miles per hour.

Storm often delayed, but rarely stopped the Christmas mail
altogether. The great crimson conveyance with its powerful
lamps, its good teams and skilful drivers kept going at all
costs.

A turkey famine threatened, and the coach-guards and
others who brought up the birds from the country, made a
good profit. The guards had a fierce time of it, for the mails

73

were their personal concern; if the coach ditched or stuck in a drift, the guard had to take a horse and ride on with the mail bags into the storm. Sometimes this meant the risk of death.

One hears again the echoes of the yard of tin (horn) twanging as through the darkness the old coach makes its way past Rydal Mount in the morning of Christmas; one sees again the faint shadow of coach lamps looming through the night mist under the hills and alongside Grasmere's lake; and one has just a touch of regret that the old romance, which in childhood days meant so much for some of us who were reared far away from the railways, can never come again with the Christmas mail.

If sheep are not brought down from the fell in the face of bad weather, many of them may be buried by drifting snow. The native Herdwick is a hardy breed, and many of them are left to winter on fellsides. It is said that these sheep were taken into Wasdale from a ship stranded on the Cumbrian coast hundreds of years ago, and from there they spread into the neighbouring Lakeland valleys. A characteristic of the Herdwick is its fidelity to the 'heaf' on which it was born. They are able to survive for days, buried under drifts of snow where, if unable to eat grass, they will survive by nibbling at their own grease-laden fleece. James Clarke wrote of their hardiness in his Survey of the Lakes *in 1787; '. . . they contrary to all other sheep I have met with, are seen before a storm, especially of snow, to ascend against the coming blast, and take the stormy side of the mountain, which fortunately for themselves, saves them from being over-blown . . .'. However, many sheep, especially the ewes, are brought down to spend the winter where the weather is less severe than on the open fell sides.*

· A Lakes Christmas ·

After severe blizzard conditions, sheep may have to be dug
out of snow drifts

While Shepherds Watched

Eleven o'clock on a white Christmas Eve, and at work
protecting a flock like the shepherds of old Bethlehem — the
memory was startling. Under the guidance of Willie, I had left
the farm at nine, and for two hours had been directed, not to
guard the flock from beasts and lions, but to drive them into a
safe position from against the onslaught of a gale. The sheep
had been Willie's care; I had driven in this grumbling ewe,
and that, as he directed, but the response had been mechanical
for my brain was impressed by vast peaks, white moors, the
silver shield of the tarn, the brilliant moonlight and the soft
radiance of the highest stars.

'Will we be out of here by midnight?' I asked Willie, and

· *A Lakes Christmas* ·

Bringing in the sheep along the southern shore of Rydal Water

great was my delight when he replied, 'Yes, if we do our job thorough.' I think that Willie wanted to hear the midnight bells just as much as I did, so we examined every shadow, hollow and rock critically.

As the minutes sped, there seemed to be an increase in silence, music no longer came from the Hall: a light here and there on the road showed that travellers were afoot. Silently we gathered more and more sheep; here and there a party trotted up without being sought for, and as the church clock tolled the hour of twelve, we stopped at the top of a long rise.

'While shepherds watched,' I rejoiced to myself as I looked across the small mob of steaming woollies in our charges. 'Merry Christmas,' shouted Willie from the other wing of the flock. And at that, the joy bells of the dale began to ring. Another Christmas had come to the wilderness, where shepherds were guarding their flocks against storm.

Soon after midnight we two returned to the farm kitchen and had the season's welcome. Then the head shepherd went out to the door where the weather glass was hung and struck a match. 'We've done well to move those sheep tonight, the glass is dropping fast.'

And Christmas dawn brought the roughest gale the farm had known for years.

from

Elizabethan Keswick

W.G. COLLINGWOOD

These extracts are from the original account books of the German miners that were kept between 1564 – 1577. The books were translated and transcribed by W.G. Collingwood and published by Titus Wilson of Kendal in 1912 for the Cumberland and Westmorland Archaeological and Antiquarian Society.

· A Lakes Christmas ·

On December 10th, 1564, an agreement was made between Queen Elizabeth I, and Thomas Thurland and Daniel Hechstetter, by which the latter pair were empowered 'to search, dig, try, roast and melt all manners of mines and "ures" of gold, silver, copper and quicksilver' in many parts of the country. The Lake District was one area that was extensively mined.

The Duke of Northumberland had held the mineral rights, but as a result of his dispute with his Queen in attempting to maintain these rights, he lost his head. Under the agreement, the Queen was to have one tenth of native gold and silver and one tenth of gold and silver ore holding 8 lb weight in cwt, and a royalty on copper and other minerals. She had 'too have the preferment in buying of all Pretious stones or pearls to be found in the working of these mines', and also rights over tin and lead. The company formed was 'The Company of the Mines Royal' and Hechstetter was the agent for an Augsburg company already involved in silver and copper mining in the Tyrol. Men working in these mines were considered to be the most skilful of their time, and it was for this reason that the German miners were brought over to develop the Lake District mines.

In the early days, the Germans were not well received in the Keswick area, being 'victims of assaults, murders and outrages' and for their own safety were advised to live on an island in Derwentwater. But as time went by, local people found work within the mining environment, the Germans married into Lake District families and became fully integrated into the area.

Accounts for the Company of the Mines Royal were issued seven times a year, the Christmas accounts being particularly important for this was the end of the financial year.

1569 Christmas Reckoning.
Rent – Roulant Walckhers widow at Gresmor – house for workmen to Martinmas – 15/-
Cristl Clarichs widow at Newlands – for room in which watchman lies and keeps all his iron and tallow – to Jan 1 – 10/- . . .
House – Bought from Mells Faschet, cabinet maker 3 bedsteads, a table and 4 forms that were Mr Thurland's, £2; also 7 ells linen at 6d for table napkins . . .
Tallow from Nicolaus Barckher in Cockhermuth £1.19.4 . . .
Wolff Prugger and Wolff Hochholtzer, master carpenters, a pair of breeches (hosen) each, as promised when the Smelthouses and the 2 stamps and all their appurtenances should be finished, and now, praise God, it is finished, £1.12.0. Also to a plumber for a lead pipe for water works, 18/- . . .
Building – T. Skott 41 days at 10d. making cartwheels . . .
Adam Stuedart carrying 2,600 slates from quarry, 15/7 . . .
Locksmith for a lantern at Smelthouses, 3/-; a lock to the timber shed, 8d; . . .
Horses – Shoeing 17 times, £1 . . .

December (Keswick) 1571
Stable (the carrier) taking 2 smelters and their wives to Keswick, 4 horses £3.6.8. 33 ells canvas to lay over the boards in the new office, 13/9; 11 ells coarse woollen cloth at 11d to hang on walls. H. Corwen for $\frac{1}{2}$tun red wine for D. and Mrs Hechstetter, £6.4.6 . . . December 24th, new cross-window in new office; mending glass in house and Smelthouses £1.6.8$\frac{1}{2}$. Clothes for our poor boy who turns the spit in the kitchen 6/8. Nailing down cloth on the office floor 2/4. Mending bellows and making a cushion 1/6. A lad for taking the carpenter to Caldbeck, 5d. Our old caretaker when she had a child baptized 3/- . . . Milady's servant bringing game 1/.

Soap 1/8 . . .

To close the statement for 1571:

Dec. 31 Bad debts – Hanns Haml, miner, dead and rotten, owed £16.18.11;

David Flitt, former English sorter, run away, £2.1.9 . . .

December 1574 (Keswick)

Dec 25. The rest of Reinburn's clothes fetched £3.2.8 from which John Wilson's and the shoemaker's bills were paid, leaving a balance of £2.13.4. . .

Israel Waltz bought a brass kettle, the earthen one not being serviceable, £1 . . .

Melort Hari Scrup Statthalter (Scrope, Lord Warden of the West Marches) at Carlisle owed us on an account for wine a balance of £3 which we could not get; but he has helped us in many ways, and can be useful still; so we write off this debt.

December 1575(Keswick)

Zipprian Schaller – for him in his illness – $2\frac{1}{2}$ lbs almonds 2/6 and after his death 5 ells linen therewith or therein to bury him; and moreover since he came to Keswick $5\frac{1}{2}$ weeks board at Hechstetter's at 5/- – £1.14.2. Since his death, his clothes have been sold and after paying his debts, there remains £1.9.0. His horse was sold to Christopher Maison £2.5.0 . . .

R Ledes the Bailey and John Bulfedt, breakfast and dinner and a quart of wine at Isel Park on business about wood 2/ . . .

Mr Braddyll, his son and two others were here bringing money and had 3 dinners, one breakfast and 9 quarts of wine – 14/- . . .

Given to the Bishop of Carlisle copper pots value 7/6 . . .

R Ledes paid Richard Wainwright for watching the wood at Isel, so that there may be no fear about it – 4/-.

Getting our little boat out of the water when the flood had sunk it – 1/6 . . .

R. Ledes going to Carlisle Assizes about people who carried off iron from Caldbeck – 9/7.

'Down at the Mill'

PAT EVANS

Charlotte was born in December, just as the nineteenth century was departing to give way to all the promise of the twentieth century. Now, aged 91, she looks back over her early years when she spent Christmas at the Mill.

These days, she lives in a terraced house near the centre of the town and has done so for the last sixty years, but she says, 'This isn't home, this is just the house that I live in.' The 'home' that she fondly remembers is the Mill House in Curwen Park, Workington. 'Home,' she says, 'is where you live as a child with your parents and brothers and grow up as a family.' Charlotte lived at the Mill House for over twenty years, until her father died in 1930 when the family had to move out, for her father had been employed as a joiner by the Curwen Estates, and their house was tied to his job. On his death their tenancy was terminated so that the house could be re-let.

The Mill House, situated between the Curwen Park and the Millfield, is even today, very isolated, and Charlotte recalls that they had very few callers. The winter evenings were spent in playing games with the family such as ludo or snakes and ladders. Other long hours were spent sewing and knitting, and she vividly remembers knitting woollen garters for her grandmother. These long pieces of plain knitting were wrapped round and round grandmother's legs, and the ends tucked in to prevent her warm woollen stockings from slipping down.

Charlotte's father and brothers were also recipients of these evening activities for they were given crocheted cotton ties which were especially shaped to go round the back of their necks, and under their collars. Another small task that Charlotte was given to do on these winter nights was to crochet around small glass marbles which were then hung like a tasselled fringe onto the tapestry which stretched along the edge of the mantelpiece.

Charlotte hates the long, dark winter nights, she always has done, and attributes this feeling to the fact that she was born into a cold, dark world from which, she says, she hasn't yet recovered.

Family preparations for Christmas began early at the Mill House when her mother started to make her own mincemeat for their mince pies; she made and iced fruit cakes and steamed Christmas puddings for hours and hours. They had no Christmas tree in the early days. Instead, the children obtained two wooden hoops from the barrels in which the greengrocer stored his fruit and vegetables. These hoops were wrapped round and round tightly with brightly coloured tissue paper and placed at right angles, one inside the other. Small ornaments and sugared mice were then hung on to the hoops as decorations. Up in the Hall yard, near the stables, was a small pond which quickly froze over during the frosty weather. Charlotte and her best friend Ada, who was the daughter of the carter employed on the Curwen Estate, used to enjoy skating on the ice. Their skates were made of wood which held an iron blade; they were then screwed on to the heels of their shoes, and away they would go, skating, sliding and tumbling across the ice.

A footpath ran beside the pond, and part way along there grew a large hawthorn tree with a big, strong branch leaning out at one side. Charlotte's father had fastened a swing to this for something else for the children to play on.

Transport – one horse power

Charlotte recalls that it was only a week before Christmas that the shops acquired a festive look, unlike today, when preparations for Christmas seem to get earlier every year. Christmas cards were sent to friends and relatives; the postman had to either walk or cycle down to the Mill House to deliver theirs. There was even a delivery on Christmas Day. The butchers' shops in the town had huge hams and large joints of meat displayed in their windows, and the aroma as you reached the doorway of many a shop was mouthwatering. Charlotte especially remembers seeing a whole pig with an orange in its mouth, displayed in a pork butcher's shop window. The fishmongers' doorways were hung with a variety of rabbits, chickens and geese, all to tempt the housewife into buying one of them for Christmas dinner.

An armful of Christmas Goose

There was no such thing as 'oven ready' birds in those days, for they were only rough plucked when delivered from the farms or other suppliers. Once the bird was bought, and taken home, then began the grisly job of cleaning and plucking. Charlotte remembers that the plucking was aided by using small pieces of burning newspaper to singe off down and small feathers. Larger feathers had to be pulled out by hand, a time-consuming and laborious job. Charlotte's family usually had a goose from one of the estate farms. The excitement of hanging stockings up on Christmas Eve was only surpassed by that brought about by early wakening on Christmas morning. Eagerly Charlotte and her brothers would examine the bulging stockings, hanging at the foot of the bed. They always received an apple, an orange, some nuts, and generally a small toy. Sometimes, Charlotte would find a pot doll to put in the wooden rocking cradle that had been lovingly carved by her father. The bed clothes for the cradle, and the clothes for the doll had been made by her mother.

Christmas was always a special time for Charlotte's family, as, for many years, her father was only allowed a day's holiday on Christmas Day, Boxing Day and Good Friday. As a special Christmas treat, all the family would sit in the lobby to watch a 'magic lantern' show. The pictures would be projected onto a sheet which was tacked on to the back of the door. Charlotte remembers the family sitting around the fire which crackled and spat as the flames burned into the bark and offcuts of wood from the joiner's shop nearby. A glass of home-made burnet wine helped to keep the cold away and bring back memories of warm summer days when they went to Wythop, near Bassenthwaite, to gather the burnets in big flour bags, or pillow-cases.

Her mother used to walk across the fields from the Mill House, to the Brewery, taking with her a milk measuring can to collect some yeast. The burnet heads were put in a crock, and covered with sugar and water. The yeast was placed on a slice of toast and then floated on top of the liquid. After several weeks of fermentation, the liquid was strained and bottled, though not corked for several more weeks. Its flavour was very like port wine, and a glass or two helped to make a pleasant family evening and to look forward to a bright and happy New Year.

from

Inside the Real Lakeland

A. HARRY GRIFFIN

A. Harry Griffin is widely known as a writer on Lakeland. For many years he wrote regular articles for the Lancashire Evening Post, *on Lakeland topics, and for over forty years contributed 'Country Diary' to the* Guardian *newspaper. Climber, walker, skier, broadcaster, but above all, a Cumbrian by birth, he is able to 'get inside' the real Lakeland and convey to a reader his own pleasure in the area. In his book,* Inside the Real Lakeland, *Harry Griffin tells of a remarkable man, Mr Lovel Mason, who liked to be first on the ice. Mr Mason was 86 years old in October 1960 when he talked to Harry Griffin about his skating experiences that stretched back to 1880.*

It is nothing new for Mr Mason to be the first man on the ice in Lakeland. He has been doing it all his life – on Rydal Water, Tarn Hows and many other places – and nowadays is understandably aggrieved if anyone gets there before him. Several years ago I once beat him to it on Rydal and have often wondered what he thought when he saw my skate marks. Officially, you might say, Rydal Water is only safe if Mr Mason says so and this is fair enough, for there can hardly be another Lakeland skater with 80 years experience behind him.

This wonderfully energetic old gentleman clearly remembers being taken on to the ice on Windermere in either 1879 or 1880 – it worries him nowadays that he cannot be exactly sure which of the two years it was. Since those far off days he has never missed the opportunity of skating on the lakes or tarns, often snatching the one day in the year when the ice has been suitable.

Mr Mason recalled that 1895 was, in his opinion, the best winter for skaters. Just before that winter began, in November 1894, the Lake District had its biggest storm of the century. Hundreds of trees were blown down, water was blown out of the lakes, falling on roads and fields as a deluge. Later, in contrast, a great quiet came over the district and then a tremendous frost, and the lakes froze, many of them from end to end. Coaches were driven across the ice of Windermere from one side of the lake to the other, and from all parts of the country, people flocked to the Lake District to enjoy the skating. Special railway excursions were run from London and the big cities to Windermere, and sometimes the ice was packed with thousands of people. There were skating races the whole length of the lake, ice yachting, moonlight skating parties and huge braziers on the ice to keep one warm. They said the ice was nearly 18 inches thick. Mr Mason particularly remembers the ice yachts, which ran on glass balls – like curling stones – and had huge sails, with a rudder cutting into the ice for steering.

Mr Mason recalled that during the winter of 1895 the people of Ambleside could hear the ice roaring and cracking in the middle of the night. As the tremendous sheet of ice began to settle down on the water it exerted enormous pressure and a

Skating on Derwentwater

great crack about a yard wide opened up from one side of the lake to the other. One evening, a man from Ambleside called Ritson, went through the crack into the water, and Mr Mason and others rushed ladders to the spot but they were too late, and the man was drowned. One of the lake steamers, fitted at the prow with ice cutters, was used for a time in an attempt to keep the lake open, but finally had to give up the struggle. And so hard was the frost that the very next day Mr Mason was skating where the steamer had been.

Mr Mason told one of his finest memories was of moonlight skating on Tarn Hows just before his 80th birthday. He climbed up the fellside after a couple of hours on the ice and saw the full moon shining through the trees on to the frozen lake. 'It was shining like a pearl, one of the loveliest sights a man could wish to see.'

Mutton and Rum Butter

What do you have for your Christmas dinner – turkey, goose, duck, chicken, or just a nice piece of pork, with stuffing and crackling and apple sauce and all the other odds and ends? Hundreds of dalesfolk have mutton, and enjoy it, for cooked properly, mutton can be just as delicious at Christmas as any other time of the year. Many years ago, the Christmas and New Year dish in nearly every Lakeland farm was a 'raised pie' – a little too rich for most of us nowadays, but worth trying if you want to taste a new flavour. It was shaped like a pork pie with the same hard crust, and inside was placed a layer of lean mutton cut up fine. You then had to fill the pie nearly to the top with currants, raisins, peel, cinnamon, and brown sugar. This was topped with shredded sheer kidney fat, and the pie was then filled with stoned Valencia raisins and had a good

Free range turkeys

89

glass of rum poured over it – or two glasses if you felt like it. The pie was baked for two hours, sufficiently long for the juice from the fruit, the fat and the brown sugar to mingle with the rum, run down into the meat and cook it into a delicious, richly flavoured dish. Try it as an experiment some Christmas time.

Most Lake District folk have some rum butter in the house over Christmas time, and many of us, of course, have it to hand throughout the year. It is always a tasty spread for bread and butter at afternoon tea. I am no cook – except at holiday times with a Primus stove – but this recipe was told me a few years ago by a Cumberland farmer's wife who had been making rum butter all her life, had won many prizes for the stuff at shows and exhibitions, and had been chosen to demonstrate her art in London. Many people, she told me, make the mistake of using castor sugar, and some of them beat the sugar to make the finished product a whitish colour, but this, she said, was not the way to make the old-fashioned rum butter you eat in the Lake Counties. Brown sugar is apparently needed – one and a quarter pound of it, according to this recipe – as well as half a pound of butter and a wine glassful of rum, best Demerara if you can get it. Another ingredient, which is perhaps the real secret of the original flavour (although some people prefer it without), is ground nutmeg – between quarter and half a teaspoonful. My informant says the right way to go about the job is to melt the butter and then stir in the sugar until the mixture begins to stiffen. This is the moment to start introducing the rum, a little at a time, and, so far as I know, the nutmeg goes with it, but I forgot to ask about that point. Perhaps it is not very important.

Having made the stuff, some people who have never eaten rum butter might well ask how they should use it. I have known rum butter used in many ways – an American friend of mine used to mix it with his breakfast bacon – and I have seen people use it as butter, and then add jam. But the way we have

ON SALE,

THIRTY-ONE HOGSHEADS

OF

Jamaica and Demarara Sugars,

Of Fine Quality.

Apply to

Mr. C. BROWN.

Whitehaven, Dec. 23, 1822.

Advertisement in the *Cumberland Paquet* Newspaper

always used it for as long as I can remember is to spread it on bread and butter. The old folk of Cumberland, however, used to spread it on cream crackers and before that on haver (or oat) bread which at one time was the staple food of Lakeland villages – that and barley bread. Originally, rum butter was only served when you were paying a social call to welcome a new baby to a friend's household. You munched haver bread spread with rum butter after you had toasted the health of the new arrival in wine.

In those old days in the Lakeland dales, hams of mutton were hung up like pork hams to smoke in the chimneys over the peat fuel, butter salted down in summer and kept for winter use in special tubs, and beer brewed from dandelions or nettles. Skim milk cheeses were made, and eaten like bread. Candles were made when there had been a big sheep killing before the winter set in.

Bread was baked in huge ovens which had first been heated with oak sticks. They were set on fire, reduced to ashes, raked out and then the bread immediately placed inside. The door was then shut and the whole of the recess round the door covered with clay to keep in the heat. The haver bread was

baked on a griddle or girdle, and a cupboard near the fireplace
was generally used for the haver meal. This was usually
prepared by the oats first being roasted like coffee and then
ground, and kept crisp and dry. Roasted oatmeal was sometimes eaten with Demerara sugar and this was possibly the
origin of butter sops, the Lakeland dish sometimes served at
Christmastime. To make this tasty dish – again taken with
your glass of wine – you melt butter and mix it into a special
sort of biscuit or bread rolled very thin and baked till dry.
Sugar is added and the finished article, I am assured, for I have
never eaten it, goes down very well indeed. Cumberland
currant cake is a delicious piece of confectionery often seen at
Christmastime. It appears in a slightly different form over the
Border. In Cumberland the currants are mixed with rum and
sugar, with a little cream added, if you have it, and then this is
used as a filling between very rich pastry.

Christmas Trees

For most people, Christmas time would seem odd without the
traditional Christmas tree. We have become so used to seeing
them in town centres, schools and civic places, not to mention
our own homes, that it is now an accepted part of Christmas.

But this has not always been the case. Before Prince Albert,
the consort of Queen Victoria, introduced the Christmas tree
to England from his native Germany the greenery to be found
in Cumbrian households would be holly, ivy and mistletoe. In

his book, *Lakeland and the Borders of Long Ago*, Walter MacIntire explained that the Germans derived the idea of a Christmas tree from the old Egyptian custom of setting up a palm tree with twelve shoots at the top. 'The palm was supposed to put one shoot each month, and the tree thus represented the cycle of the year. It was hung with offerings. It is possibly on account of this Egyptian origin that the original German Christmas tree was a pyramid of pasteboard framework adorned with paper streamers, to represent foliage.'

Christmas trees grow in numbers in the extensive Forestry Commission plantations of the North Lakes. These forests extend from near Ullswater with the Greystoke Forest, to the plantations on the slopes of Skiddaw and across Bassenthwaite Lake to cover both sides of Whinlatter Pass. Further south in the county, forestry development in Ennerdale and Eskdale also come into the North Lakes Forest District.

Planting of the Whinlatter Forest began on the 9th December 1919. Over the years this Forestry development has increased and extended its role to provide an area of recreation, which people can explore and enjoy. At Whinlatter there is a Visitor Centre with a series of exhibits and displays. Mike Pearson is Head Ranger (Recreation) and is in charge of the Centre which attracts about 80,000 visitors a year. He explained the commercial production of Christmas trees which are sold at Whinlatter each year.

The five species of tree that are sold as 'Christmas Trees' are Norway Spruce, Sitka Spruce, Scots Pine, Lodgepole Pine and Silver Fir. There are no nursery beds at Whinlatter for the development of young trees, so two-year-old trees are brought in from specialized forest nurseries to be planted three feet apart in suitable areas. Odd spaces in the forest will be utilized for this planting, although it is important to have easy access to a road for transporting the felled trees when they are harvested. Ground under high-power electricity cables is

Harvesting Christmas trees at Thirlmere

ideal, for there is no danger from the trees growing to a great height as they are cut down when they are from five to seven years old. They can also be planted in good viewing areas along recreational trails, because the trees do not grow so high as to obscure the view.

Areas of forest where the soil is poor are good for growing Christmas trees, for the lack of nutrients in the soil helps to restrict the trees' growth and produces bushier specimens. The trees are managed, in that they are trimmed to a good shape which is always a prime requirement of the buying public. Their other demand is for a tree that will keep its needles, and in this respect, the traditional tree, the Norway Spruce, is a poor tree to have indoors as it sheds its needles very rapidly in spite of any treatment that it may be given. The Sitka Spruce

94

is more suitable as it holds its needles longer. This tree is easily recognized by the green-blue sheen of its foliage. It has a disadvantage in that its needles are extremely prickly, although that may be seen as a useful deterrent to curious little fingers.

The two species of pine trees are becoming increasingly popular as Christmas Trees for they can hold their needles for up to three months, although it is unlikely that anyone would want to put that characteristic to the test. The disadvantage of a pine tree is that the foliage tends to be rather sparse for it is quite difficult to produce a bushy pine tree.

The Silver Fir is by far the best species for a Christmas Tree. It holds its needles well, the foliage has a nice soft feel, and yet it is firm enough to hang ornaments and decorations on its branches. It can also grow to a bushy shape.

Once a decision has been made and a tree bought, thoughts turn to the aftercare of the tree in the home. Forestry advice is to delay purchase of a tree as long as possible, so that it has the best chance of retaining its freshness. When the tree is taken home, it should be given a good shake to remove any loose needles, and then the bottom one or two inches should be sawn off the trunk. This opens up the 'pores', and the tree should be stood in cold water immediately. After a period of a few hours, the tree can be put in its Christmas container and, provided it is kept watered, it does not really matter whether it stands in sand, gravel, or stones; in fact, scrunched up newspaper is ideal. Soil is not good as it tends to clog up the pores and prevents the tree from absorbing water. The tree needs about a pint of water of a day, although this may gradually reduce over the Christmas period, and will vary according to the surrounding temperature conditions. Normally, coniferous trees begin to lose their needles quite naturally when they are more than five years old, due to age and lack of light penetrating through the dense foliage of the forest. The modern problem of acid rain can result in a reduction of this time, for it has been discovered that its effect is causing needle loss from two- and three-year-old branches of the trees.

About 1,000 trees are sold in Whinlatter each year. They are available from the last week in November, though usually trees sold then are to schools, hospitals, or hotels and are the larger and more mature trees. Schools are encouraged to bring parties of children to choose their own tree, and watch it being felled. They are always asked to 'apologize to the tree' before it is cut down, and accompany its fall with cries of 'Timberrrr'. Rooted trees are not sold at Whinlatter, mainly for economic reasons, but also it has been found that successful replantings are uncommon.

Relatively few trees remain unsold, although there is always a last minute dash by someone to buy a tree. The felling of trees is continuous throughout the period of demand, but those that are left are taken to areas of the forest where re-cycling of brash and foliage from other felling is already taking place. This is a vital process where a natural breakdown occurs to return much needed nutrients to the soil.

Confused by this variety of tree that is available? Maybe it's much simpler just to think about a 'Christmas Tree'.

Most people apparently forget about all the advice they have been given and choose a tree they like the look of. One fact does emerge that continually surprises the forestry staff: after the marital rows that go on over the choice of Christmas trees, why do they see the same couples year after year?

from

Rogue Herries

SIR HUGH WALPOLE

Many visitors come to the Lake District expecting to see tangible evidence of Walpole's fictitious family, for so realistically did he portray all the characters in their lakeland setting.

His descriptions of locations are so graphic that one can actually discover the settings, and through imagination join members of the Herries family in their many activities. The mid-eighteenth century in the valley of Borrowdale is the setting for their Christmas festivities.

That was the happiest evening they had yet had in Borrowdale. The hall was bright, the fire leaping, the candles burning, the floor shining. Wilson had hung three old flags that had been buried in the oak chest, one of crimson with a white cross, one of faded purple and one of green. Whose flags? From what wars? No one knew. The holly was thick with red berries that year and hung from the rafters. They could hear the bells ringing from the Chapel above the splash and crackle of the fire. . . .

Next night, Christmas night, they were invited to Statesman Peel's. It was not as it was in most parts of England

97

where at Christmas time, the Squire was King of the Castle and his subjects were graciously bidden to enjoy his hospitality with a proper sense of his grand benignancy and their inferior peasantry. In Borrowdale every Statesman was master of his own house and owed allegiance to no one. Every Statesman's house was open on Christmas night to all the world, rich and poor. There were the guests, indeed, who had their special places there, but the doors were wide open to the stars and the line of friendly hills and the hard-frosted road.

Peel's kitchen this night was a place of splendour. Its warmth and colour, its happiness and hospitality, stretched to the farthest heavens. Glaramara and the Gavel looked in at the windows, the Derwent rolled its waters past the door, and every star scattered its light over the roof-tree. . . .

The front door was covered with a low porch, the entrance from which was called the 'thresh-wood' or threshold, and on

Winter in the Borrowdale Valley

this thresh-wood crossed straws, horseshoes and so on, were laid to hinder the entrance of witches. From this there was a broad passage through the house called the 'hallan'; sacks of corn were deposited here before market-day, pigs were hung after killing, and there was a shelf over the door where sickles hung and carpentry tools were laid.

In Peel's house the hallan opened straight into the 'downhouse'. This was in his case the great common room of the family, the place of tonight's Christmas Feast. . . . Francis Herries, arriving with his children David, Mary and Deborah, found that already everything was in a whirl. Peel himself greeted them magnificently, standing his six foot four, splendid in his dark coat of native fleece and buckskin breeches, and Mrs Peel, stout, very red of face, in russet, all the little Peels (and there were many) gathered together behind her.

Many were already dancing. It was a scene of brilliant colour with the blazing fire, the red berries of the holly glowing in every corner, old Johnny Shoestring in bright blue breeches and with silver buckles on his shoes perched on a high stool fiddling for his life, the brass gleaming, faces shining, the stamp of the shoon, the screaming of the fiddle, the clap-clap of the hands as the turns were made in the dance – and beyond the heat and the light the dark form of the valley lying in breathless stillness, its face stroked by the fall of lingering reluctant snow. . . .

The door would open and the snow blow through in little impatient gusts and all the valley would pour in with it. The room was crowded now against the wall and in the corners. The ale was passing round, and voices were loud and laughter ferocious. But everyone behaved in a seemly fashion: a dignity, that seemed to radiate from the grand figure and quiet hospitality of the host himself, pervaded the place. Only – as Francis Herries could feel – he could sniff it in the air – there was a kind of madness behind the dignity, something that belonged to the witches and old crippled warlocks, to the naked shapes playing under the stars above Seatoller, to the broomsticks flying dimly like thin clouds towards the moon.

Suddenly there was a cry: 'They coom. They're here.' It was the 'Play-Jigg'. This was the drama in verse played by the actors who, tonight, were passing from Statesman's house to Statesman's house.

Johnny Shoestring ceased his playing, the dancers vanished, the centre of the room was clear. Packed against the walls now were the bodies and faces, legs and backs. There was whispering and tittering, but quite clearly in the immediate silence could be heard the hiss of the snow hovering down through the open chimney on to the fire.

They came forward. . . . The Master of Ceremonies . . . introduced his little company, Old Giles, a bent old man with a long chin, Pinch, a clown, a stout and jolly fellow, a husband and a wife, and young Go-to-Bed who at once in a high shrill treble introduced himself:

> 'My father is old and decrepit,
> My mother deceased of late,
> And I am a youth that's respected,
> Possessed of a good estate.'

The old couple did a little dance of joy at this, and then Pinch the clown came forward and asked young Go-to-Bed if he wanted to increase his fortune. Of course young Go-to-Bed was eager, so Pinch introduced him to Old Giles, who said he would show him how to make money out of nothing. This young Go-to-Bed was delighted to know, so Old Giles told him that he must have his arse kicked a dozen times by friend Pinch, and then he must put his head in a bucket of water and then must sit up a night alone in a churchyard: all these things young Go-to-Bed performed to the infinite delight of the audience, especially in the churchyard when Pinch, dressed as a painful ghost, emptied a sack of flour over young Go-to-Bed and set the dogs on to him.

The 'Jigg' ended in a grand dance and in this the audience soon joined. Go-to-Bed, his face white with flour, led off with Mrs Peel, and Peel took the Old Lady, and soon all the room was turning to Johnny Shoestring's music.

Miracle in the Market Place

CARSON I.A. RITCHIE

During the Middle Ages, and for long after, Christmas in Cumbria was not just a period of mirth and good cheer. It was the high point of the cultural year in which the guildsmen and their wives would combine to perform an annual miracle play which they had written themselves, as well as building the scenery. The musical accompaniment was provided by musicians of the various guilds. The principal centres for miracle plays in Cumbria were Carlisle and Kendal. All the plays were religiously based, though solemn representations of the great mysteries of faith were leavened by the introduction of comic interludes concentrating on local humour.

The choice of a play depended on the wishes of the majority of the guildsmen and their wives, and also the backers who would have to foot the bill for what was frequently a very expensive production. There are references to payments for sweeping the streets clear of snow to allow access to the ponderous floats. A really ambitious cycle of miracle plays, such as those which were staged in Cumbria, might include 'the whole of the Old and New Testament, with interludes not warranted by Holy Scriptures but put in as light relief'.

Cumbrian miracle plays were however certain to include a

Nativity, if only because Cumbria was essentially a pastoral county. Now in a Nativity Play, it was the shepherds who were continuously on stage from first to last, who had the longest speeches, and the most dramatic parts to play.

Anyone watching a Christmas play at Carlisle or Kendal would have no difficulty in identifying with the actors who played the shepherds, and thus setting foot on that ladder between Earth and Heaven that the Miracle Plays were written to provide. The actors would be speaking a broad Cumbrian, their clothes possibly borrowed from real shepherds or certainly of local material and in the style of the region.

The shepherds dressed in Kendal Green, would sit down to the kind of snack eaten on the hill pastures; sausages, pig's trotters, cold tripe, a sheep's head soused in ale, sour milk, newly baked bread, butter and new laid eggs, onions, garlic and leeks, a pudding, a Lancashire oat-cake, and the famous Cumberland ale.

Though strict realism might have suggested that most shepherds only got a hunk of bread in real life, it must be remembered that amongst the other purposes of the miracle play, there was 'the benefit of the commonwealth and prosperity of the city'. Consequently the audience, after watching the shepherds eat their lunch on the stage, would go off with a sharper appetite to the taverns themselves, thus promoting trade for the innkeepers.

Everything in a Nativity Play had to be doctrinally correct. Though not necessarily written by churchmen, Miracle Plays would be overseen by one. There was usually good scriptural authority for everything that took place in a play. Thus Joseph goes off to look for two midwives to help Mary with her confinement. These midwives are not mentioned anywhere in the New Testament, but they are in the Apocrypha, which was felt then to have much the same authority as Scripture.

So strongly was the religious message put across in a Miracle

Play that an old man of Cartmel, talking with the Puritan vicar of Rotherham, John Shaw, was able to recall the introduction of the topic of Salvation in 'a play at Kendall, called Corpus Christi's play'.

Not just the religious message, but the background had to be authentic. Shepherds talk about treating their sheep with herbs such as Pennywort, Flinter Fanter, Fetterfoe, Henbane, Horehound, and Egremont.

Though unfortunately all the text of the Cumbrian plays is lost, it is possible to reconstruct, from comparisons with other dramatic centres, the sort of show that would have been put on at Kendal. Each play was confined to a separate float, prepared and acted by a particular guild. This need not be a trade guild. Corpus Christi, for example, which put on the play that the old man at Cartmel remembered so well, with its realistic details such as the crucifix on stage and blood that appeared to run down, was a religious fraternity.

These floats would be dragged through the streets, they would stop at fixed points, before the door of a church for example, and the representation would take place. There were as many plays and floats as there were guilds prepared to undertake the trouble and expense. Sometimes guilds would agree to share expense on a particular float and play. The Glaziers and Painters, for example, might undertake to get ready the angel who appeared to the shepherds, the Wright and Slaters to prepare the *Gloria in Excelsis* sung in Heaven. The Vintners might enact the arrival of the Magi, the Mercers or the Goldsmiths, the Massacre of the Innocents with which the Christmas Story closed. Some ambitious plays needed the co-operation of no fewer than five guilds.

While the cost of production was considerable, many guilds felt that they would get the best value for their money if they put on two representations, one at Christmas, and one at Whitsun. The floats, the costumes, the stage scenery and properties, were all expensive to store and keep in repair as well as to construct in the first place. In some play centres, arsenic had to be mixed with the paste-board that made up the masks to prevent the rats eating them in the interval between representations. The 'pageants' as the floats were called, were always two-storeyed, the upper storey being the part where the actors usually appeared, the lower serving as the green room and the dressing room. Ladders and trapdoors enabled the actors to descend or ascend, and there were trapdoors and lifts for dramatic entrances or exits.

The pageant had an open top, rather like a sightseeing bus nowadays, so that even if anyone were unable to get to the show itself, they could still admire the actors in their costumes as they were drawn past by manpower or horses. Rather like a bus again was the route followed by the floats. The first performance would certainly be given at the High Cross, before the Mayor, after heralds had proclaimed the beginning of the performance. Once the floats had begun to circulate through the crowded streets – no easy matter, one would feel – word was passed by messengers to say whether or not the play ahead had ended, and its pageant was moving off.

Not merely did everyone look forward to the Miracle Plays in Cumbria. Many of the townsfolk must have spent a large part of the year saving up to pay their contributions. Every member of the guild was taxed for a contribution, masters and journeymen paying more than apprentices, and sometimes 'foreigners' or non-guildsmen paying as well. Some of this money got back into the guild if it was paid out to actors and actresses. The players were paid for attending rehearsals, and also given their meals on the day when they were rehearsing or performing. Sums paid varied according to the difficulty and also unpopularity of the part. Pilate and Herod were both unpopular, demanding roles which needed experienced performers who could ask high pay.

In contrast to Kendal, Christmas dramatic festivities at Carlisle depended much more heavily on the 'Boy Bishop'. This was a special festival held on or around Innocents' Day, when a chorister, sometimes the oldest and most hard-working of the choir, would act as if he were bishop, wearing robes and mitre and carrying a crozier. Often the regalia of the boy bishop was made specially for him and of considerable splendour.

In return for acting in a play specially written for him, sometimes in Latin, and giving a 'sermon', which again was written for him, taking part in dances, processions and singing, he received special fees.

In spite of strenuous efforts by the Puritan clergy and their sympathisers to suppress them, the Cumbrian Miracle Plays were still being enacted well into the seventeenth century. A note in the Carlisle Tailors' Guild Book for 5th January, 1659 reads as follows:

> *It is ordained and appointed by the said guild that upon Corpus Christi day, as was the old use and custom beforetime, the whole Guild with the banner be in St. Mary's Church-yard at the ash tree at ten of the clock in the forenoon, and he that comes not before the banner be raised to come away, pays sixpence for each offence.*

At Kendal too, the plays lasted into the seventeenth century, though there had been an attempt to stop them in 1586, unless the aldermen were unanimously in favour of putting on the play. Thomas Heywood noted in 1612 that continuing the play was not just a matter of dramatic interest:

> *Kendall holds the privilege of its fairs and other charters by yearly stage plays.*

Weever, writing about 1631, refers to the:

Corpus Christi play in my country, which I have seen acted at Preston, and Lancaster, and last of all at Kendall, in the beginning of the reign of King James I, for which the townsmen were sore troubled, and upon good reasons the play finally suppressed, not only there, but in all other towns of the kingdom.

The Snow

JOHN RICHARDSON

John Richardson is little known within the boundaries of Cumbria, and yet he was quite a remarkable man. He was born in 1817, was educated at the village school, and with no further advanced education, he became schoolmaster in 1858. Prior to this, he had been a builder, and in 1845, along with three other men, he took on the task of re-building what was then known as St John's Chapel. He was regarded as a quiet, resolute, kind hearted man who valued the Cumbrian dialect as being 'honest and straight-forward'. He wrote much prose and poetry in dialect, and his first book was published in 1871 when he was aged 54.

He died in 1886 aged 68, and is buried in the

· A Lakes Christmas ·

*churchyard of the little church in St John's in the Vale,
next to the church he had helped to build, and close to the
school where he was master.*

It com doom as whist an' as deftly as death,
O' soond nut a murmur, o' air nut a breath;
Flake reacin' wi' flake. Oh 'twas bonny ta see
Hoo it curver't up moontain, an' valley, an' tree.
Doon, doon it com floatin', sa white an' sa clear,
Ivvery twig, ivvery leaf, hed its burden ta bear;
Ivvery dyke, ivvery house, ivvery rough cobble wo',
Hed its blossom, its reuf, or its copin' o' snow.
Doon, doon it com floatin' sa swiftly an' leet,
Seun t'landscape was white as a tribble bleach't sheet;
An't' grund 'at was leatly sa' starv't like an' bare,
Was lapt in a mantle, a feut thick or mair.

Ther coald stores exhaustit, t'leet cloods floatit by,
An' pure white as t'earth was, as deep blue was t'sky;
Far sooth Sol appeared, majestic an' breet,
His rays wake an' slantin' an'guiltless o' heat.
Threw ower that white picter a splendour an' sheen,
'At twice in a lifetime can rarely be seen.
Ivvery crag, ivvery dyke, ivvery snow-laden tree,
Was an object worth gaan a lang journey ta see;
Neah art, tho by t'cleverest artist could show
A picter sa' grand as that landscape o' snow.

T'grim demon o' winter, wi' envy hofe craz'd,
To see a scene sec a scene i' December-upraist
A fierce wind fra t'north, 'at whissel't an' rwoar't,
An' dreav t'snow i'blindin' cloods dancin' afwore 't.
Fra't fells into t'valleys, doon whirlin' it went,
It fand ivvery crack, ivvery crevise, an rent;

View into St John's in the Vale

Through t'mortarless wo's, in auld hooses, it sed,
Fwok waken't to finnd theirsels snown up i' bed.
While creelin' by t'fences for shelter, t'poor sheep
In t' snowdrifts war hap't up, aye, ivver sa deep;
For days an' days after, t'auld shipperds wad post
Off wi't cwollies, to hunt up odd sheep 'at war lost;
An' some nivver fund war till spring, when leate on
They frozen turn'd oot efter t'last snow was gone.

from

A Christmas Party

SUART'S ALMANACK 1896

Suart's Almanack was a little journal, which kept local inhabitants in touch with what was happening in the area. It also included such national information as details on the Royal Family of the day, postal regulations, taxes, licences and even patent fees. Local tradesmen used its pages to advertise their goods and services:

'Balls and Parties supplied on reasonable terms.'

'New and second hand harness always in stock.'

'Dresses to fit perfectly.'

The following extract describes a party which took place in a town on the fringe of the Lake District. It represents the way in which daughters of well-to-do people in these northern towns, were given the opportunity to be launched on the 'Social Scene' – the northern middle class equivalent of being 'presented at court'.

There was a Christmas party, a few years ago, and a birthday festival combined, – an evening of mutual enjoyment, of indulgence in small talk and tittle tattle, of love-making and jealousy, and a little scandal, of course.

110

The invited guests themselves assembled do not always 'dwell together in unity', but take a delight in noticing every little personal defect in one another, and comment thereon with a severity that is purely choice scandal. . . . Then there's the dude who is always in full evidence at these select parties, and who having attained great proficiency in the art of flattery and foppery, mashes other people's sweethearts, flirting here and there, and making himself a general nuisance. . . .

Mary Ann, who had been in existence exactly twenty one Christmas Days, was about to be presented to the world by her mamma through the agency of one of these select parties.

The large drawing room was artistically decorated for the occasion, festoons of ivy were hung in divers forms and arranged in fantastic shapes around the room intersected with branches of spruce and slips of mistletoe.

There was a numerous gathering present, and great care had been taken in the selection thereof by Mary Ann and her ma; their stations in life were considered, and their pedigree summed up, so to speak as to their length and limit. All this was considered essentially necessary to keep Mary Ann and her ma on a par with well-bred people. . . .

Many of these favoured mortals were young and interesting girls, who were making their début in society, innocent of the world's ways. So peculiarly innocent were some that they never thought of a 'kissing bush', never dreamt of its existence, and even when the older heads were observed smirking and casting sly glances behind their fans, they never seemed to notice it, but paraded under its very centre and received the affectionate salute marvellously well. . . .

Mary Ann had her young man there, Philip Grimwigg. He was a handsome fine fellow, and would have been exquisite in the eyes of the ladies had he been less in love with himself. Then Walter Scott had some good points too, and there was much innocent argument among the females as to which of the

twain was the most pleasing. Others spoke somewhat dispa-
ragingly of the favourites and advocated the salient points of
their own particular fancies, and they all blushed respectfully.
The rivalry began to be keen and to wax as the night wore on,
and jealousy showed signs of becoming one of the guests. . . .
Dancing is a general favourite at these parties, so after the
'kissing bush' had had its innings, the fascinating waltz
whirled the assembled guests into dreamland.

The ladies were charming. Their faces in the first flush of
youth showed signs of innocent enjoyment, and the young
men, whose enthusiasm was somewhat reserved at first, began
to be more attentive and to throw more energy into the
labyrinthine dance, and love was making raids in various
directions and creating fearful havoc in the hearts of the young
debutantes. . . .

Walter's darling, Tottie, had completely captivated Philip
Grimwigg, and had generally brought him to his knees. They
were seen stealing away from the general company, whispering
and casting fitful glances over their shoulders as if looking for
someone they didn't want to see; then they slipped behind the
thick velvet curtains that hung in front of one of the bay
windows. There wasn't much room, but they made it do.
Mary Ann had observed the whole proceedings with watery
eyes for she was sorely smitten.

Now Tottie, never in a moment imagined that anyone in
that select company would be so mean as to look behind the
curtain, gave full vent to her emotions in whispers and sighs.
Throwing their arms about each other's neck, she burst out
with, louder than was necessary, 'Dear Philip – could this
sweet moment but last for ever, oh how happy I would be if –'

But that sweet moment didn't last ten minutes. Mary Ann,
who was rather sensitive on matters of this kind, had had quite
enough of it, and with a wrench pulled the curtain down, and
faced the lovely pair with quivering lip and flashing eye.

Great Heavens. Would it not have made the Angels weep? Her own Grimwigg clasping Tottie's wrist with a grip that would have made any ordinary woman scream.

She could stand it no longer.

'Traitor – insulting, mean reptile,' she faltered between gasps. 'Philip Grimwigg, I don't care THAT for you, you contemptible mole – not THAT – nor THAT.' And she snapped her finger and thumb in his face each time she uttered the word 'that'.

'And as for you madame, take THAT,' and she hit Tottie across the face with her fan, and stalked away – freezing.

Philip and Tottie were somewhat piqued at this show of temper, and being slightly in the minority thought it best to retire with all speed.

The party soon broke up after these events had taken place, and the guests scrambled home two by twos, wondering if such episodes were frequent. . . .

The Shape of Gifts to Come

BARRY KNOWLES

Racking your brains as to what to buy friends and relatives for Christmas this year? Barry Knowles has some

suggestions for you which are a shade unusual, to say the least.

An Ambleside man who is well known in the area for his cartoons that poke gentle fun at the Lake District way of life, Barry Knowles is a regular contributor to the Cumbria *and* Dalesman *magazines and is the creator of the* Sheep's Eye View *series of books that are published by the Dalesman Publishing Company. He also contributed a cartoon strip to the* North West Evening Mail, *a Barrow paper, on a fairly regular basis.*

Edible Wainwright

No longer need you set out on a Wainwright walk and feel peckish. The set of guide books is now available printed on quality rice paper so you can follow the route, climb the fell, and enjoy a tasty snack at the summit. Dust wrapper in cling film to retain freshness.

Budgie Backpack

Why leave Joey at home when you can clip him handily on to your backpack with his very own travelling cage?

Comes complete with emergency cuttlefish rations and gingerbread flavour millet.

Floating Mintcake

At last, a taste of Lakeland to enjoy at bath time. No more soapy sweetmeats thanks to these mintcake-size bath floats. Suitable for white, brown and even chocolate covered varieties. Works equally well in lake or tarn.

Broll-o-Phone

Stuck in a downpour and
nothing to do? Now's the
time to catch up with all
those important business
calls. Aerial retracts as
weather brightens.

Pack-o-Clamp

Specially designed for the Lakeland
landlords whose bar becomes
impassable during invasions of
backpackers who dump their
belongings all over the inn. If the
annoying luggage is not removed
within five minutes, Pack-o-Clamp
sounds klaxon and sets fire to the
whole thing.

Jet-Alert

Avoid shocks to the nervous
system with this new device which
gives ten seconds warning of
approaching low-flying jets and
automatically clamps on earmuffs –
they retract after shock waves
abate. Tested at Farnborough air
show. 'I didn't hear a thing,'
claims satisfied user.

The Scents of Lakeland Sprays

Relive those heady Cumbrian holiday moments with these handy aerosols for you to spray and enjoy at home. Choose from the following aromas: Sheep Fair, Beer Tent, M6 Traffic Jam, Haverthwaite Steam Trains. Ozone-friendly.

Rubik Rock

A genuine piece of Cumbrian rock, handily smashed into a hundred pieces for you to re-assemble at home. Hours of fun for all the family and a useful paperweight when completed.

Phoney Photos

Say goodbye to tired leg misery. You need no longer climb Scafell to have your photograph taken at the summit. Simply poke your head through this authentic-looking backdrop and,

click – you're a mountaineer. Exciting waterski action back-drops also available.

Visi-Stickers

The Busy Visitor just doesn't have the time to carve his name on every tree and rock in the county. These handy self-adhesive stickers attest to your presence at all beauty sites.

Slate-o-Fax

The first Filofax set made of genuine freshly-mined slate. Be the envy of your office colleagues. Contains sections for holiday snaps. Useful travelling wheels fitted for ease of transport.

Sheep-Shoo

Picnic misery is a thing of the past thanks to this handy 'loud-barker' which convinces marauding, scavenging sheep that you have a sheep dog in your party. Your sandwiches are safe and there will be no more unsightly sheep droppings on your picnic cloth.

Christmas Weather

We may be conditioned by too many repeat showings of 'White Christmas', or the snow painted on decorated windows; or is it the snowmen of snowscenes on Christmas cards that makes us look back with nostalgia to what Christmas weather used to be like?

To be honest, I can't remember many white Christmases; plenty of wet and windy ones, and quite a few when the day was crisp and sunny with a hard frost.

For an account of a really hard frost, it's worth looking

· *A Lakes Christmas* ·

A quiet corner of Ullswater

back almost four hundred years to an occasion when Ullswater was frozen over – an event noted in the parish records of Watermillock near Ullswater, in 1607.

In the yeare of our Lord 1607 was a marvellous great frost which contynued from the first day of December until the XV th day of February after.

Ullswater was frozen ower and so contynued from the VIth day of December until the XXII day of February followinge. So strong that men in great companies made a common way up the same from John Barton's dore to Fewsdaille Wyke. And men of Martindaill carried shepe up the same on at Bartons and at Sharrowsande. Men went up the same water and over it with horses loaden with corne. Upon the VIth day of January the younge folkes of Sowlby went into the mydst of the same water and had a minstrell with them and there daunced all the after Noone. On Shrove Tuesday being the IXth day of February at Weathermillock was a boone fire builded on the Ise and matches of shotinges shott and a pott with aill drunke thereupon by (many) – Edward Wilson, Anthony Rumpney, Frances Rumney, John Castlehow, and others.

Anthony Rumpney and Frances Rumney were forebears of Tom Rumney of Mellfell.

from

History of Cumbria

W.M. HUTCHINSON

The months of December and January are frequently very windy in the Lake District. One particular wind, the Helm wind, is prevalent in the eastern part of Cumbria. W.M. Hutchinson in his History of Cumbria *published in 1796 describes it in the following way:*

The name of 'helm' seems to be derived from the Saxon, and implies in our language, a 'covering'. Its appearances have

been that of a white cloud resting on the summits of the hills, extending even from Brough to Brampton; it wears a bold broad front, not unlike a vast float of ice standing on edge; on its first appearance, there issues from it a prodigious noise, which in grandeur and awfulness exceeds the roaring of the ocean. Sometimes there is a 'helm bar', which consists of a white cloud arranged opposite to the 'helm', and holds a station, various in distances, sometimes not more than half a mile from the mountain, at others, three or four miles; sometimes it is in breadth a quarter of a mile, at others, a mile at least: this cloud prevents the wind blowing further westward. The sky is generally visible between the helm and the bar, and frequently loose bodies of vapour or small specks of clouds are separated from the helm and the bar, and flying across in opposite directions both east and west, are seen to sweep along the sky with amazing velocity. When you arrive at the other side of the bar cloud, the wind blows eastwards, but underneath it is a dead calm or gusts of winds from all quarters. The violence of the wind is generally greatest when the helm is highest above the mountains. The cold air rushes down the hill with amazing strength so as to make it difficult for a person to walk against it.

It mostly comes in gusts, though it sometimes blows with unbated fury for twenty four hours; and continues blowing at intervals for three, four, five or even six weeks.

Weather Lore of the Lakes

Christmas time is often the time when traditional sayings and idioms come to light and, as with most areas, there are many proverbs and anecdotes peculiar to the Lakes. The following selection might well be heard in the days prior to Christmas.

A green Christmas makes a fat churchyard.

If the sun shines not on Christmas Day
The apple crop will surely fail.

A far off bruff [halo round the moon]
Tells of a near hand storm.

Of a keen wind – It's fit to skin a paddick [toad]

If October ice will bear a duck
At Christmas will be sludge and muck.

Winter. Cald Winter.

GIT REDDY ME LADS!

PATIENT.   DOCKTER.

DOCKTER : " Well me friend, what's up with you ? "

PATIENT : " Oh ! I's turbly plagued wee Brown Kightess, Teethwark, Torpled Liver, Appyditus. Nasty Taste, Colliwobbles, Housemadenee, Hassma, Bad Dreeams, an Cald Feet, ah fairly can't keep warm e bed."

DOCKTER : " Well, me man, Medicine in your case is not needed. take my advice, go at once to the Bowness Fent Shop and buy warm Winter Clothing."

DOCKTER'S FEE, 21/-.

Patient pays it like a man ; fits hissel up as ordert, and in a few days lowps aboot like a kittellin.

Lambs Wool Pants and Vests, fra 2/11.

Men's Winter Shirts (all makes) well made, fra 2/6.

Cardigan Jackets, full size, fra 2/3.

Collars (all shapes) including " Bertie Willies," best makes, 6d.

Ties, Stockings, Socks, Cuffatees, Scarfs, Caps.

Also a few Second-hand Box Hats, Wellington Boots, en Swalla-Taled Cooats, suitable fer Funenals and Weddins, fer Hire. Terms Moderate.

FRANK ROBINSON sells the best Half-crown Shirt in England.

Some suggestions for keeping out the winter cold, 1906

from

The Verge of Lakeland

W.T. PALMER

*During the 1745 attempt by Prince Charles Edward
Stuart to regain the English throne, his army marched
south through Cumberland and Westmorland. Possession
of Carlisle changed hands between the Highlanders and
the Hanoverian troops, as they sought control of the
garrison town. This extract from W.T. Palmer tells of the
last 'invasion' of Cumbria in mid-December 1745.*

The last time Penrith Beacon was fired in earnest was in
December of 1745. Early that month Prince Charles Edward
Stuart at the head of an army of Highland clans crossed the
rivers Esk and Eden, captured the city and castle of Carlisle
without firing a cannon shot, then marched through Penrith
and Kendal to Lancaster, Preston, Manchester and Derby. The
Hanoverian garrison of Carlisle, after laying down their arms
in the market place, marched up the Eden valley by Appleby
and Brough on their way to York. The country people of
Cumberland and Westmorland offered no help to the Scots.

Towards Carlisle from the north showing the Cathedral and
Castle

Their militia, 700 strong, had melted away at Carlisle, just, as
thirty years before, it had dispersed when the Stuart army
marched towards Penrith Moor.

This time the Stuart army, taking Carlisle, left a weak
garrison there, a force reduced further by a draft sent towards
Manchester and Derby, and was unable to keep order even in
the city, under the guns of the Castle. According to one
report, the draft of forty were attacked at Lowther by '30
stout, brave, young men from Penrith, well armed'. One of
the rebels was killed, and nine taken prisoners, who were sent
immediately up the Eden valley to General Wade's headquarters.

There was excitement when rumour came that the Scots had
been defeated in a battle somewhere in the south, that the
survivors were retreating towards the Border. On Saturday,

December 14th, a company of Stuart hussars, 110 to 120 in number, under the Duke of Perth, arrived in Kendal. Their story was that they were travelling to Scotland to bring up more men and carrying despatches. An anonymous letter sent to the Mayor said that the Duke of Cumberland had smashed the main force, and that these were the only survivors of the column. 'A person in woman's clothing' riding in a chaise, was claimed to be Prince Charles himself in disguise, trying to get back to Scotland.

Anyway, the Duke of Perth, his company and the chaise had a cold official reception. Hodgson, in his *History of Westmorland* gives details of the mob stoning the troopers, who had to fire, wounding four persons, two of whom died. In the melee in Finkle Street, four Scottish soldiers were taken prisoners, and at Stramongate bridge one horseman was shot, seriously wounded, and taken to Shap where he died,

. . . from which place they proceeded that afternoon to Eamont Bridge; but perceiving Penrith Beacon on fire, they inquired the reason, and being told it was to raise the country, and that all the hedges from that place to Penrith were lined with armed men, they returned to Shap, where they halted for the night. . . .

On Sunday the Duke of Perth tried to reach Scotland along the east side of the River Eden, for it was obvious that no small party like his could force the road to Carlisle garrison through hostile parishes. From Shap the hussars rode to Clifton, and crossed the Eden at Temple Sowerby bridge; then went by Culgaith to Langwathby moor. The Penrith men had crossed the river farther north, and there was pistol fire between the forces.

The cavalry had to turn south again, and were mobbed through parish after parish until they got back, by Morland and Reagill to Shap. Even here the pursuit was keen, but at Orton the cavalry had left the mob behind. They refreshed themselves, and got back to Kendal on the Sunday night.

The Highland foot had reached Kendal on the 15th. They levied a fine on the town for the death of their hussar, and when the bulk of their army reached Penrith on the 17th they threatened to burn that place for its share in the 'Sunday Hunting'. Of course the armed mob had vanished in the meantime, and the 'scouts' of General Wade's army, 120 strong, which had stiffened the resistance, had crossed the Eden at Gamblesby, and were well out of reach of punishment.

Probably Kendal had suffered more than Penrith from requisitions, horses, money, arms and goods, and the people were more annoyed on that account. The Kendal register contains the following entry: '1745, Dec.16, John Slack kild by ye Scots'.

from

Dorothy Wordsworth's Grasmere Journals

Many people feel that Dorothy Wordsworth's writing deserves as much recognition as that achieved by her famous brother, William. The journals that she wrote while at Grasmere give a fascinating insight into the landscape

and its people. Small incidents are recorded in great detail, and the reader, especially if one is familiar with the area, can feel almost drawn into the Wordsworths' company.

These extracts drawn from her journal writings for December 1801 allow us to share the Christmas period in the company of Dorothy, Mary and William Wordsworth.

The editor, William Knight, states, 'The journals contain numerous trivial details which bear witness to the "plain living and high thinking" of the Wordsworth household.'

Wednesday Morning, 9th December . . . Mary and I walked into Easedale and backwards and forwards in that large field

The track leading from Grasmere into Easedale, from a mid-nineteenth century engraving

under George Rawson's white cottage. We had intended gathering mosses, and for that purpose we turned into the green lane, behind the tailors, but it was too dark to see the mosses. The river came galloping past the Church, as fast as it could come; and when we got into Easedale we saw Churn Milk Force, like a broad stream of snow. At the little footbridge we stopped to look at the company of rivers, which came hurrying down the vale, this way and that. It was a valley of streams and islands, with that great waterfall at the head, and lesser falls in different parts of the mountains, coming down to these rivers. We could hear the sound of the lesser falls, but we could not *see* them. We walked backwards and forwards till all distant objects, except the white shape of the waterfall and the lines of the mountains, were gone. We had the crescent moon when we were out, and at our return there were a few stars that shone dimly, but it was a grey cloudy night.

Saturday, 12th . . . Snow upon the ground . . .Helm Cragg rose very bold and craggy, a Being by itself, and behind it was the large ridge of mountain, smooth as marble and snow white . . . The snow hid all the grass, and all signs of vegetation, and the rocks showed themselves boldly everywhere, and seemed more stony than rock or stone. The birches on the crags beautiful, red brown and glittering. The ashes glittering spears with their upright stems. The hips very beautiful, and so good . . . I came home first. They walked too slow for me . . . Mr Clarkson came in before tea. We played at cards. Sate up late . . .

Monday, 14th December – Wm. and Mary walked to Amble-side in the morning to buy mouse-traps . . . Sate by the fire in the evening reading.

Friday, 18th December 1801 – Mary and Wm. walked round the two lakes. I staid at home to make bread. I afterwards went to meet them, and I met Wm. Mary had gone to look at

Ambleside *c.* 1830. Artist, G. Pickering

Langdale Pikes. It was a cheerful glorious day. The birches and all trees beautiful hips bright red, mosses green.

Sunday 20th December – It snowed all day. It was a very deep snow. The brooms were very beautiful, arched feathers with wiry stalks pointed to the end, smaller and smaller. They waved gently with the weight of the snow.

Monday, 21st being the shortest day, Mary walked to Ambleside for letters . . . I stayed at home. Wm sate beside me, and read *The Pedlar*. He was in good spirits, and full of hope of what he should do with it . . .

Tuesday, 22nd . . . As we came up the White Moss, we met an old man, who I saw was a beggar by his two bags hanging over his shoulder; . . . He was 75 years of age, has a freshish colour in his cheeks, grey hair, a decent hat with a binding round the edge, the hat worn brown and glossy, his shoes were small thin shoes low in the quarters, pretty good. They had belonged to a gentleman. His coat was blue, frock shaped, coming over his thighs. It had been joined up at the seams behind with a paler blue, to let it out, and there were three bell-shaped patches of darker blue behind, where the buttons had been. His breeches were either of fustian or grey cloth, with strings hanging down, whole and tight. He had a checked shirt on, and a small coloured handkerchief tied round his neck. His bags were hung over each shoulder, and lay on each side of him, below his breast. One was brownish and of coarse stuff, the other was white with meal on the outside, and his blue waistcoat was whitened with meal.

Wednesday, 23rd – . . . A broken soldier came to beg in the morning. Afterwards a tall woman, dressed somewhat in a tawdry style, with a long checked muslin apron, a beaver hat, and throughout what are called good clothes. Her daughter had gone before, with a soldier and his wife. She had buried her husband at Whitehaven and was going back into Cheshire.

Thursday, 24th – Still a thaw. Wm, Mary, and I sate comfortably round the fire in the evening, and read Chaucer. Thoughts of last year. I took out my old journal.

Friday, 25th – Christmas Day. We received a letter from Coleridge. His letter made us uneasy about him. I was glad I was not by myself when I received it.

Monday, 28th of December – William, Mary, and I set off on foot to Keswick. We carried some cold mutton in our pockets, and dined at John Stanley's where they were making Christmas pies. The sun shone, but it was coldish. We parted from Wm. upon the Raise. He joined us opposite Sara's rock. He was busy in composition, and sate down upon the wall. We did not see him again till we arrived at John Stanley's. There we roasted apples in the room. After we had left John Stanley's, Wm discovered that he had lost his gloves. He turned back, but they were gone . . . We reached Greta Hall at about $\frac{1}{2}$ past 5 o'clock. The children and Mrs C. well. After tea,

Dunmail Raise in the early nineteenth century

message came from Wilkinson, who had passed us on the road, inviting Wm. to sup at the Oak. He went.

Tuesday, 29th – . . . We turned out of the road at the second mile stone, and passed a pretty cluster of houses at the foot of St John's Vale. The houses were among tall trees, partly of Scotch fir, and some naked forest trees . . . We crossed a bridge just below these houses, and the river winded sweetly along the meadows. . . . As we ascended the hills it grew very cold and slippery. Luckily, the wind was at our backs, and helped us on. A sharp hail shower gathered at the head of Martindale, and the view upwards was very grand – wild cottages, seen through the hurrying hail-shower. The wind drove, and eddied about and about, and the hills looked large and swelling through the storm . . . We dined at the public house on porridge, with a second course of Christmas pies . . . The landlord went about a mile and a half with us to put us in

133

the right way. The road was often slippery, and the wind very high, and it was nearly dark before we got into the right road. I was often obliged to crawl on all fours, and Mary fell many a time. A stout young man whom we met on the hills, and who knew Mr Clarkson, very kindly set us into the right road, and we inquired again near some houses and were directed by a miserable, poverty-struck looking woman, who had been fetching water, to go down a miry lane. We soon got into the main road and reached Mr Clarkson's at tea time. Mary H. spent the next day with us, and we walked on Dunmallet before dinner, but it snowed a little. The day following, being New Year's Eve, we accompanied Mary to Stainton Bridge.

Logs to Burn

For those who still have an open fire and the facility to burn the traditional yule log, the following rhyme may give guidance as to the best sort of log to burn.

Logs to burn, logs to burn
Logs to save the coal a turn.
Here's a word to make you wise
When you hear the woodman's cries.

Oak logs will warm you well
If they're old and dry;

· A Lakes Christmas ·

Larch logs of pine wood smell
But the sparks will fly.

Beechwood fires burn bright and clear
Hornbeam blazes too,
If the logs are kept a year
To season through and through.

Holly logs will burn like wax
You should burn them green;
Elm logs like smouldering flax
No flame to be seen.

Pine is good and so is yew
For warmth through wintry days,
But poplar logs and willow too
Take long to dry and blaze.

Pear logs and apple logs
These will scent your room;
Cherry logs across the dogs
Smell like flowers in bloom

Birch logs will burn too fast
Alder scarce at all.
Chestnut logs are good to last
If cut at the fall.

But ash logs, all smooth and grey
Burn them green or old,
Buy up all that comes your way
They're worth their weight in gold.

Lakeland and the Borders of Long Ago

WALTER MACINTIRE

Walter MacIntire was a regular contributor of articles to the Cumberland News. *He wrote on all sorts of Cumbrian matters for over fourteen years. Born in Settle in 1870, he turned to journalism after trying his hand at teaching. He died in 1944, and the book, which is compiled from a selection of his work, was published by the* Cumberland News *in 1949 as a tribute to him. The following piece describes some of the old Christmas customs of Cumberland.*

. . . In many farms, Christmas Day was the only occasion in the year when the new and – in the eighteenth century – expensive luxury of tea was enjoyed by the family and farm hands. It is interesting to note that Anderson, 'the Cumberland bard', in the 1820 edition of his poems, makes one of his characters, an old man speaking in the days gone by, attribute the degeneration of the Cumberland statesmen to such practices as the drinking of tea! After tea, the rest of the day was passed in playing 'lanty' or some other card game.

The festival began on Christmas Eve with a strange meal composed of frumenty or firmity, a thick liquid concocted of milk boiled with wheat or barley and seasoned with spices. The frumenty was accompanied by Yule cakes – heavy and richly spiced buns upon which was rudely represented the sign of the Cross. A mighty cheese, in some households of the Whillimoor variety – 'lank and lean, but cheap and clean' – adorned one end of the table, and the master of the house, before cutting off the guests' helpings, always cut the figure of the Cross upon its surface. After this meal, which was washed down with spiced ale, the rest of the evening was passed in games, of which the most usual was 'bobbing' for apples. The apples, which had to be 'bobbed for' or caught in the mouth by the players, were attached to one end of a pole hung by a rope in a horizontal position; to the other end of the pole was tied a lighted candle.

The apple in Celtic lore had always had a religious significance, and the maintenance of a light, here represented by the candle, was in pagan times associated with the mid-Winter season of the year. The same remark applies to the Yule log or clog which was placed upon the fire at Christmas. It was considered a lucky omen if the new Yule log was lighted from a portion of that of the preceding year. We seem here to have survival of the primitive necessity for keeping a fire continually burning, 'a Vesta's sacred flame'.

Another old Christmas Eve custom in Cumberland was the eating of nuts, which had to be cracked with the teeth without regard to the risk of adding toothache to the dangers caused to the digestion by the copious consumption of frumenty, Yule cakes and cheese. Christmas Eve, on account of this practice was sometimes called 'Nutcrack Night' . . .

A Christmas custom, now happily abolished, was the

slaying of wrens. These unfortunate birds were slain on Christmas Day, and on the following St Stephen's day the bodies of the victims were carried in triumphal procession, suspended in a framework composed of two hoops set at right angles to one another. The name of the wren in many European countries signifies 'Hedge King', and the Druids are said to have represented the bird as king of an evil race which had been transformed into birds, hence the prevalence of this cruel and useless practice.

Perhaps, however, the most interesting survival of Christmas festivities is that of the representation of the Christmas play by 'guisers' or mummers. The Cumbrian form of this play is very brief. A youth enters and asks the company present to show a light to illumine the coming play. There enters Farmer Dick with a big stick and King George. They fight and the farmer falls, while King George remorsefully cries, 'Five pounds for a doctor! Ten pounds for a doctor! Twenty pounds for a doctor!' This tempting offer attracts Dr Brown, 'the best old doctor in town', who can cure:

'The itch, the pitch, the colic and the gout.'

He restores Farmer Dick to life. The play is explained variously as representing the death of Summer at the hand of Winter, and Summer's eventual re-birth, or as the death and resurrection of the god or goddess of the harvest, but the purpose of the mummers is fully disclosed by the final words spoken by Johnny Funny, the leader of the band:

'Here comes I Johnny Funny,
I'm the man who collects the money,
It's money we want and money we'll have,
If you don't give us money we'll sweep you all out.'

We end Christmas Lore with mention of the decoration of houses till Twelfth Night with festoons of holly, ivy, yew and

mistletoe, the 'all heal' of Celtic tradition, or of the provision in some houses of dolls made of pastry or gingerbread with currants for eyes and buttons. These perhaps represent the old harvest goddess and are akin to the 'Kern Baby' of harvest time.

The Cumberland Paquet *of December 1774 also bears testimony to the celebrations that went on in Lakeland at Christmas.*

As an instance of the great festivity which prevails at this season, a correspondent informs us, that in the township of Buttermire (which consists of only 16 families), there are 17 fat sheep killed; from each of which sheep, 50 pies are to be made; so that the number of pies to be destroyed this Christmas, in the township of Buttermire, amount to *Eight Hundred and Fifty.*

from

Mountain Lakeland

TOM BOWKER

To quote the author, this book is 'one man's view of mountain Lakeland after over thirty years out and about on the fells in all seasons and in all weathers'.

· A Lakes Christmas ·

The extracts used indicate what it was like in those days when walkers were dependent on public transport for getting to and from the fells; the post-war years before the days of the 'universal motor car', days with which I can easily identify, having had to walk weary miles at the end of a day on the fells, having missed the last bus. . . .

High Street

My first ascent of High Street was during a Christmas leave whilst I was enduring National Service. My wife Joyce and I disembarked from a Ribble bus at Troutbeck Bridge. We walked to Troutbeck, and climbed High Street by way of the Roman road zigzagging up the flank of Froswick. I remember it was clear and the views were superb, the snow was crisp underfoot and there was a nippy wind. Our intention was to follow the ridge all the way back to Garburn Pass but by the time we got to the dip below Froswick I was knackered, and stunned Joyce by suggesting that we followed the path flanking Froswick, Ill Bell and Yoke. The highly-trained infantryman who was an integral link in the defence of the free world had knees that felt as though they had been injected with blancmange, whilst the typist-cum-housewife was eager to add more summits to the day's bag. She relented, however, and we traversed, but even so it was dark before we reached Garburn Pass. The rough road down to Troutbeck was icy in patches and despite the aid of clinker nails I kept disappearing into the outer darkness in a shower of sparks and profanity. The road miles to Windermere seemed endless, to me, before we reached a Windermere cafe and I was resuscitated by tea, pie and chips. In truth I was an orderly room clerk in a training depot and in the way of army clerks was skilled at avoiding all forms of physical activity. The only exercise I got was cycling a mile every day to the village bakery for hot pies and cream cakes for the RSM and the orderly room sergeant.

Whatever it says for my fitness, the fact that we were able to catch a bus from Lancaster, walk around sixteen miles and have time for a leisurely meal before catching the last bus back, says a lot for the then public transport – I doubt if it could be done now.

Blencathra

Up Sharp Edge and down Narrow Edge was the route we took the first time I climbed Blencathra. Cloud was well down the mountain as was the snow line and as we traversed the line of the path across the steep bowl of the mountain we had great fun hurling ourselves down the slope and practising emergency braking with our ex WD ice-axes, those who had them. We somehow missed the path to Scales Tarn and finally reached the crest of Sharp Edge via a gully on its northern flank. Those of us with ice axes fully accepted our responsibilities for those without and proceeded to chop armchair-size steps up the steep slope to the summit ridge, in the process virtually denuding this corner of the mountain of snow. So enthusiastic were we that a party coming up behind us almost decided to turn back because of the snow avalanching down on them from out of the murk. The summit of Blencathra is broad and grassy and has an east – west dip bisecting it. Obviously, from a distance and to the perceptive among us, this is the seat of the saddle. We ploughed down into the dip and up the further side until suddenly a subtle change in the surface under our boots warned us that this was cloud, not snow – we were virtually on the lip of the cornice overhanging the Threlkeld face. The 'Narrow Edge' of Hallsfell was exciting as we kicked and slashed enormous traversing steps around the 'crag-work'.

We knew that when we got down we would have to walk back to Keswick to catch the bus home. It had been decided that John would take one of us to Keswick on his pillion while the rest started walking.

This ferrying tactic became more common practice as more

motorbikes began to appear in our ranks. Not an Oriental amongst 'em however. Norton, Triumph, AJS, Ariel, Royal Enfield, Douglas, BSA, Dominators, Gold Stars, Tiger 100's — a litany of vanished glory. It was incredible that we survived the burnups and dicing. There was no M6, no Kendal bypass, no compulsion to wear crash hats — just the old treacherous A6, and the narrow roads of Lakeland.

Great End

Great End in winter is Lakeland's Eigerwand. Its north-eastern aspect, its crag base altitude of over two thousand feet, its triumvirate of gullies, its broken grassy buttresses, all combine to retain ice and snow for long periods. The use of crampons on British hills was not considered sporting when I started climbing. The Great End gullies are long and when iced must have required prodigious stamina and not a little time in those pre-crampon days. . . .

Inevitably, there have been accidents, several tragic. This grim aspect of winter climbing on Great End was starkly illustrated to me on the one occasion I attempted it one New Year's weekend. After a remarkably mild Christmas there had been a sudden cold snap. The sun shone, there was not a breath of wind, but the cold was intense and distant Derwentwater was crusted with grey ice. The mountain was a hive of activity, the frozen crags and gullies packed with brightly coloured blobs of humanity and there was a handful of tents pitched at the head of Grains Gill. There had, however, been an accident in Central Gully a few days before and a great fan of avalanche debris, still blotched ominously pink, spewed from the gully mouth. It ruined my day. As I stamped up the steep chute of Cust's Gully my imagination worked overtime. I felt the sudden lurch of snow underfoot, the helpless cartwheeling tumble, the battering rocks. By the time I pulled myself over the cornice I was lathered in sweat and it was not all from physical effort.

The Christmas Carol

GWENDOLEN PAGET

Browsing through some old parish magazines, I came across a copy of the parish magazine of St Michaels, Workington, dated December 1903. It held the following article that gives some interesting background information on the Christmas Carol. The reference to the carol's profitability must be known to every youngster that comes knocking on one's door in the intervening weeks between Bonfire Night and Christmas Day.

The Carol is of very ancient origin. The word seems to have meant songs intermixed with dances, but it was afterwards solely applied to songs of festivity, pious or otherwise, at various seasons of the Church's year – though more particularly at Christmas.

The word Carol is derived, so it is said, from 'Cantare' to sing, and 'rola', a pious interjection, and it is thought that in olden days the bishops sang these sacred songs amongst their clergy – Warmstrey, a sixteenth-century writer said: 'Christmas Karils, if they be such as are fit for the time and of holy and sober composures, and sung with Christian sobriety and piety, they are not unlawful, and may be profitable, if they be sung with grace in the heart.'

But the Carol was not only a pious song of rejoicing. It was sung to usher into table that standing Christmas dish of our ancestors – the Boar's Head, at which a regular ceremony took place. There are several records of carols being set or ordered, amongst churchwardens' accounts and from other sources. They became so popular that in 1521, Wynkyn de Worde printed a set of them, and this is the earliest known collection. In the Book of Expenses of Queen Elizabeth, Queen of Henry VII, is the following entry,

'William Comyshe received 13s. 4d. for setting of carrall vpon Christmas-day in reward.'

In 1562, John Lysdale had a licence for printing 'certayne goodly carowles to be sunge to the glory of God.' One of the oldest carols in existence is believed to be the 'Gloria in Excelsis'.

It is given in its old wording.

When Cryst was born of Mary fre
In Bedlem ht fayre cyte
Angellis songen wt mirth and gle
in excelsis glia.

Herdure beheld ps angellis brygt
To hem apperyd wt gret lygt
And seyd goddis sone is born thys nygt
in excelsis glia

Ps kynge ys comyn to save kynds
. . . . In scriptur as we finde
. . . . for thys song have we i mynde
in excelsis glia

. . . . lord for thy gret grace
. . . . is yn blys to se thy face
Where we may syng to pe solas
in excelsis glia.

The Other Side of the Altar

HOWARD ASKEW

In the hustle and bustle of activity during the weeks that lead up to Christmas Day, it is very easy to forget the fact that this day is one of the great days of celebration in the calendar of Christian churches.

145

· A Lakes Christmas ·

Christ's birthday has not always been celebrated on the 25th December as the following account from the Whitehaven News *of the 25th December 1941 explains.*

'Many, no doubt are unaware of the fact that a few centuries ago the birth of Christ used to be celebrated in the month of January, also in February. Since then it has been altered to the 25th day of December, and that date has now become stabilised. Shortly before Christ was born, all went out to be taxed, everyone into his own city, and Joseph, along with Mary went up from Galilee, into Judea, unto the city of David, Bethlehem. It is obvious that this did not occur in the month of December. Owing to the conditions of the weather in Palestine at that time of year, it would be impossible to travel from place to place. The Scriptures are silent regarding the date of the miraculous birth, but they do reveal that the Lamb was slain on the 14th day of April. The death of Christ is of much greater importance to the Christian Church than His birth as a child. Whilst the birth of Christ is a historical fact, no one has any Biblical authority for stating that He was born on the 25th of December.'

In churches of many different denominations throughout the Lakes area, Christmas celebrations begin with an act of midnight communion.

This account of the Christmas Eve service is seen through the eyes of a young acolyte of an Anglican church in Cumbria.

Although it is called the 'Midnight Mass' the service actually starts at eleven-thirty and we have to be there a little earlier to get changed into our robes, and to set out the chalices. Although this is the same procedure that we go through each time we are 'on duty', it does feel different on Christmas Eve.

We arrive at the vestry one by one; some early, some late, but every one in high spirits. The usual feelings we experience before a service are heightened by the general mood of tension and expectancy. We are all excited, proud, and a little nervous at the prospect of participating in the joyful celebration of the birth of Jesus. The Vicar wears a special stole, and a richly embroidered cloak to complement the altar decorations, which are changed to represent the different seasons of the year, or the special services. He says a special prayer of thanks to God for granting us the opportunity to help in His service, and asks for guidance so that we don't make too many mistakes. We then join the choir, and enter the church in procession.

There are many more people than usual at this service. They all stand as we enter, led by the 'Crucifer' who carries the cross. On either side are two young acolytes, who carry each a candle to light the way of the cross. I follow next, then the choir, Curate, lay assistants and finally, the Vicar.

This is the difficult part as far as the Crucifer is concerned, for he has to walk, at just the right pace, to lead us round the church to get us to the Sanctuary as everyone finishes singing the processional hymn. We've learned to ask how long a hymn lasts when we know there is to be a procession round the church, then we can get the timing right and avoid having to suddenly speed up, or slow down in the middle of a hymn.

We all feel relieved once the service has actually started. This is especially true for the young acolytes who may only have taken part in two or three services since their confirmation in November. When I first started, I was still quite nervous until I'd made all the mistakes possible; then I realized that it didn't really matter because the congregation never noticed, and God doesn't really mind as long as I do my best.

I have very little to do until it is time for the 'Gospel' when the Vicar reads the familiar story of the birth of Jesus. He reads this from the middle of the church. I have to carry the Bible in procession and hold it at the right height for him to read. I often wonder where to look as I stand there with everyone looking towards us. Should I look down at the Vicar's bald patch; or try to look angel-faced towards the Altar? The leather bound Bible is heavy as the Vicar looks for the right page; I hold steady, and after the reading we return to the Altar.

Then follows the 'Peace', when everyone shakes hands, a sign of peace. I accept the money from the collection brought to the Altar by sidesmen, taking great care not to scatter the well filled plates and then we prepare for Communion. The elements of wafer and wine are brought up by two members of the congregation, a form of audience participation. The gate to the Sanctuary is closed as preparations are made. This is a hard part for the young acolytes who have to stand with their heavy candles in front of the Altar, while the Vicar blesses the bread and the wine. They are glad for the opportunity to kneel, for a long stand in hot robes, holding a heavy candle, can leave one a little faint.

The Vicar has his own Communion, and then gives it to us before the rest of the congregation come to the altar rail to receive their bread and wine.

We watch everyone come up for communion. Some are unsure, some have come straight in from the pubs; they watch others, trying to work out what to do. Slow moving lines of people shuffle forward to take a place at the altar rail while the choir fills the church with Christmas music.

After Communion, I have to 'wash-up'; that is rinse the vessesl and the chalices with wine and water. All this liquid is then poured back in a chalice and is drunk by the Vicar. We clean these vessels properly after the service, eager to get

changed quickly and with a Merry Christmas to everybody, get back home to bed, to wait for Santa.

Most people attending the Midnight Service are adults and older children, but there is a special service for young children that is sometimes held on Christmas Eve. It starts with the blessing of the crib and is followed by a Carol service, and finally the children receive their Christingle. This involves the children going up to the altar rail to receive an orange banded by a red ribbon. A lighted candle is on top of the orange into which four cocktail sticks are speared with dried fruit and nuts. Each element of the Christingle is symbolic; the orange represents the world; the red ribbon, the blood of Christ; the candle, the light of the world; and the fruit and nuts, the fruit of the earth. The church lights are dimmed, and the only illumination comes from the flickering candles.

A few years ago, this was my favourite service in the whole of the church year, irreverently looking forward to roasting the raisins and nuts in the candle flame. Orange light glows on young faces as they carefully cup the orange in their hands, as they walk in procession round the church. With the words of 'Away in a Manger' echoing into the heights of the church, a hundred candles burn with the same joy and delight as that illuminating the faces of a hundred children.

It is a celebration of light and life and music. From any side of the Altar, the church is a wonderful place at Christmas; filled with the happiness and joy in which God means men to live at all times; but sadly is all too often forgotten when the New Year comes, and the tinsel taken down.

Boggles

Before the days of radio, television, pubs and discos, Cumbrians would spend the long December evenings in the social round of visiting each other's houses to play cards, knit, or just sit round the fire exchanging stories of unusual happenings. Many of these stories would be about 'Boggles' – that strange ghostly thing that haunted many lonely areas of the county. Unlike the 'Dobbie' a friendly ghost that farmers liked to have about the place, there was nothing amiable about a 'Boggle' which could appear in virtually any form. Jessica Lofthouse, in her book North Country Folklore *describes them in the following way:*

'A boggle is an often faceless creature, a light, a ball of fire, a ghostly shape, a phantom hound or bull, or calf or red hen, or black cock. They often had to keep watch over treasure. They could uncover the graves of the dead . . .'
No wonder the 'Boggle' assumed such frightening proportions, and reasssurance was sought in explanation.

The following tales, attributed to the 'Boggle' and its antics are taken from the Cumberland Paquet *of 22 December 1774, and from a paper presented by the Revd J. Bulkeley to the Cumberland and Westmorland Archaeological and Antiquarian Society, in 1885.*

A remarkable affair happened the last week nigh Buttermire in this county. A boy who was apprentice to a shoemaker in the country, had been sent on a piece of business about five or six miles from home; on his return, his mistress enquired the

reason for his staying so long; the boy told her that he had the greatest difficulty in passing the bridge of a certain river in the neighbourhood; that he had been almost blown over the side of it, and that he was positive he would have been drowned, had he attempted to cross it again; for which reason, he had taken a longer road to avoid it. This he mentioned several times, and seemed very glad that he had escaped it. After he had warmed himself, he was sent upstairs to call his shop mates to dinner, and to change his clothes. The family had sat sometime at dinner, but the boy had not appeared when repeatedly called upon, one of them ran up to look for him, and found him sitting on one of the steps, strangled in the crupper of a saddle which hung in the staircase. It appeared to the coroner's inquest almost unaccountable how he could be suffocated in that posture; but no intention appearing by the boy's conduct, of laying violent hands upon himself, they brought in a verdict of accidental death.

Boggles are very common. There must be few parishes without one or two. But the belief, even in boggles, has much waned, and there are not a few who laugh at them, and try to account for them. Three winters ago the north of this parish was troubled by a boggle which contrary to the habits of its class, trotted about here and there in places many miles apart, raising unearthly cries. The more timid were afraid to venture out of their houses after sunset, and the hair of one upland farmer, who heard the cry so stood on end that his hat was 'fair lifted off his head.'

It is now believed that it was a badger which had got out of Naworth woods. A boggle is known to haunt a narrow lane with steep banks between the Irthing and Birkhirst. A man I know was passing up this lane in pale moonlight, and, though of a sceptical turn as to such things, was well nigh converted into sudden belief, when he observed a remarkable human animal standing at the upper end of it, 'a most delicate monster' . . . for it had sometimes one, sometimes two heads, and its distorted body swayed from side to side, and put out feelers like a cuttle fish. It was with great effort that he nerved himself to walk up to it, but he was much relieved, and his scepticism was more than re-established when he found it was 'just a woman a' hiding a' hint a man'. But let it not be supposed that boggles are always of this poor, explicable kind. Not such was the woman in white in Askerton Park who 'on one occasion stopped a rider, laying hold of the bridle, so that both horse and rider were powerless to proceed till a promise had been given which, if divulged, would result in the death of the rider. She then vanished'.

But at nearly the same place, this, or a companion, appeared in a very different shape to a farmer's wife, for, as she herself told me, it ran up the whip 'for all the world like a duck'. This may have been the same boggle that is said to have 'always' ridden behind Mr Maughan, the late rector of Bewcastle, when coming home this way, as far as the Kirk Beck, the boundary of the parish. The same clergyman is said to have gone one night into the church and to have 'seen a figure looking at him from the gallery, which with a scream, vanished'.

I have heard of no recent instance of exorcism in the case of an unpleasant and obstinate ghost, but an old man, now dead, dimly told me of the High Stone Moss boggle, seven years there and for seven years before at Scaleby Castle, and how 'they had some sort of a priest till't,' but it was of no use, for the boggle 'hadt' scriptures as fast as he had'.

Not long ago it would seem to have been the general belief that, on the death of any person, his spirit, with the form and colour of a faint flame, passed along the 'burial road' to the church, and up it to where the coffin would rest, and thence to the grave,. . . . Once, in Bewcastle, the horse drawing a

hearse stopped short in the road, and refused to advance a step in spite of all blows and coaxing. Then someone told how he had seen a dead-light leave the road at that spot, and take a short cut across the fields. There was nothing for it but to take the coffin out of the hearse, and carry it across the fields to where the eye-witness stated that the dead-light had rejoined the road. Thither the horse quietly proceeded, and, the coffin having been placed on the hearse, quietly drew it to the church. . . .

from

Christmas in a Fellside Community

BARBARA SMITH

Happy New Year

When Christmas is over we look forward to New Year. Living so near the Scottish border, 'Auld Year's Nicht' is an excuse for 'a good leet oot'.

Friends drop in for supper, the pubs are packed full and everyone manages to get to 'the do' in the village hall in time for Auld Lang Syne. The poor harassed doorkeepers manage to cope and are given a drink from the first footers' bottles. New Year wishes and kisses are exchanged and the dancing at one end is stopped while a space is cleared for a young man doing a step dance. He produces a hunting horn from his pocket which he promptly blows.

The dancing continues in its glorious uncivilized way, mellowed by a mixture of alcohol and goodwill. Everyone enjoys themselves as only members of a long established fellside community can. People come and go on their way 'first footing', toasts are drunk and a mouth organ is played as granny and grandad dance a jig. The menfolk are reluctantly dragged off home to let folk get to bed.

Returning to work with New Year lambing

Next morning 'I just want a cup of tea' is the cry at breakfast as everyone tries to drag along doing the morning's work, while the aspirin bottle gets a good trade. A few people continue to come and go, but the celebrations draw to a close. 'We're awe stoke-fed,' folk say, 'glad to get back to plainer fare – bacon and tatties, scones and cheese.'

from

Lakeland and the Borders of Long Ago

WALTER MACINTIRE

First Footing

In West Cumberland it was customary for the first foot to bring a piece of coal into the house and place it on the already burning fire. Perhaps due to the decline of the coal industry, and the growth of central heating, this tradition of placing coal on the fire has died out. Nowadays, although the incoming New Year is still celebrated in many Cumbrian households, it usually takes the form of a visiting round of friends' households, and can go on until the early hours of the morning, when a lighted window indicates whether or not there will be a welcome.

Food, drink and warm hospitality are all enjoyed to the full, in the knowledge that there will be a price to be paid on the morrow.

Walter MacIntire records in his book Lakeland and the Borders of Long Ago *how first footing was part of the Christmas celebrations and that Christmas Eve was the night frequently chosen for First Footing.*

One of the young men of the party leaves the house about midnight and returns for re-admission. He must have no money in his pocket nor must he carry a light. He then has the privilege of kissing the ladies present.

An interesting point about this ceremony is that in the Cumberland district the favoured beau must be dark haired, whereas in some other parts of England he must be fair. This perhaps harks back to the early days of society when marriage with girls of one's own tribe was forbidden and brides had to be sought elsewhere. A red-headed man was debarred from becoming a first footer, either on account of the tradition that Judas Iscariot was red-haired, or in our border district, because of our proximity to Scotland. In some places the custom of Hogmanay still survives. Hogmanay is a corruption of Greek words meaning 'holy month', and the word in various forms is used in many European countries. Groups of children go about singing 'Hogmanay, Hogmanay, Give us cakes and cheese and we'll go away'. A dole of cheese and oaten cakes called 'farls' is distributed among the singers. As elsewhere, contributions of food and money were also demanded by parties of waits and carol singers.

from

Mountain Rescues Recalled

'SALLY BOWE'

For many years 'Sally Bowe' was a member of the Keswick Mountain Rescue Team; a lone woman among a team of men, she proved herself their equal and came to be regarded as 'one of the lads'.

The book is a collection of true stories of rescues with which she was involved. Like all emergency services, the mountain rescue teams expect to be called out at any time. The Christmas holiday period, with the risk of bad weather, results in a busy time for the Lakeland teams.

Volunteers to the Rescue

We had been anticipating trouble all day. It was a Sunday afternoon in early January. Heavy snow had been falling on the tops and white puffs of cloud covered the summits. In the valley, however, it was merely dull and cold. Judging by the number of cars parked in the valleys there were plenty of walkers out and about. The call came at about 3 p.m. Our team was asked to assist a neighbouring team who, it seemed were trying to deal with several incidents simultaneously. This is the usual procedure. We learned later that nine separate incidents had occurred at the same time. All the Lake District teams were involved.

At the Traveller's Rest in Grasmere, some confusion was in evidence. A young policeman seemed to be in charge. 'We want as many people as possible up at the tarn,' he was saying.

'What equipment do we need?' we tried to ask.

'I don't know,' he shouted. 'I've just been told to get as many people as possible up to the tarn.'

Shrugging our shoulders, we took a stretcher, rope and basic equipment, and set off up the track.

Twenty minutes later, I was aware of a change in the atmosphere. Lifting my eyes from the ground, I could see the snow coming. Ahead of me, only one team member was visible. He too was looking around and seeing me close behind, waited.

'That looks nasty,' I said. He agreed and we looked around for others. There was a girl some distance below and behind us. We decided to wait for her. Three was better than two in the conditions that we soon realized would hit us.

We hadn't long to wait. Within minutes the full force of the blizzard arrived. We were blinded by the swirling snow as it stuck to our eyelashes. The wind gusted strongly, alternately pushing us along, and impeding our progress. Backs bent, we pressed on, the girl finding the going difficult. During the times when we were able to speak, we were gradually able to piece together her story. She had been walking past the Traveller's Rest when she heard the policeman shouting about the accident and asking people to go up to the tarn. She had felt obliged to volunteer her help. As she was now finding it difficult to continue and the job was clearly beyond her capabilities, we tactfully suggested it might be better if she returned to the valley. Eventually she was forced to agree and reluctantly began to retrace her steps. The two of us plodded on and reached the col. The snow stopped falling as suddenly as it had started. Several groups were visible in the vicinity of the tarn. We joined one with a radio to await instructions. We learned that four walkers had fallen about a thousand feet from Fairfield and we hurried across to where we thought they might be. More people arrived to help and soon each casualty had a small band of rescuers. One man was beyond help. His body was taken down. A young child who had fallen with him was virtually uninjured, despite having fallen the same distance. He was carried down, bruised and badly frightened. A third man had a fractured thigh, which was splinted before he was taken down to Patterdale. Our casualty had a severe chest injury, and as he was lying nearer the Grasmere side of the mountain, we decided to evacuate him that way.

By now, most stretchers were in use and we found ourselves forced to wait for one which we were told was on its way. We made the man as comfortable as possible and tried to reassure him. As we waited, we became conscious of the fading light. A party of instructors and students from an outdoor pursuits centre arrived with the stretcher. Fortunately, they also had ropes and as they had been climbing, ice axes and crampons. Such had been our rapid and unprepared ascent that we had none. Having secured the casualty, we started on the short uphill stretch to reach the Raise Beck track. With volunteers, the carry was far from easy, but we were grateful for their equipment and assistance without which we could have undertaken nothing. In the beck on the descent, the only way to stay upright was by holding on to the stretcher. This was impossible when we hit ice under the snow and we landed flat on our backs. Although we couldn't see the ice in the dark, we found this was an infallible means of detecting it. I picked myself up for the umpteenth time, calling to the volunteers to watch their step.

It took over an hour to make our painstaking way down to the road. Throughout, we had talked to the casualty who repeatedly thanked us. Quite suddenly, we turned a corner and found ourselves able to sledge rather than carry the stretcher. Below and to our left we could see headlights and a blue flashing light. We made that way, telling the casualty that he was nearly down and would soon be more comfortable. 'I'm fine, I'm fine,' he coughed. We reached the waiting ambulance and handed over to the crew. We heard later that the man was discharged quite fit some weeks after. While we waited for the transport we collected together the equipment and thanked the volunteers, without whom no rescue could have taken place. A short time later, wet and tired, we were drinking hot soup in Grasmere. I looked at the personal equipment I had taken with me and realized its hopeless inadequacy. To my permanent kit I added a small torch and a pair of instep crampons.

Even rescuers learn something after each rescue.

from

Donald Campbell

D. YOUNG-JAMES

Donald Campbell spent Christmas and New Year 1966 – 7 at Coniston, where he stayed for over two

months preparing an attempt on the world water speed record. His objective was to be the first man to achieve a speed of 300 m.p.h.

Campbell had been born to speed, for his father, Sir Malcolm Campbell, had also held the world speed record in his boat Bluebird.

Alongside his record attempt, Donald Campbell and his chief mechanic Leo Villa were developing a new speed boat. An American firm had promised financial backing for this venture if Campbell broke the world water speed record by January 1st, 1967. As the days ran out, tension and frustration grew at the team's headquarters at the Sun Inn, Coniston.

While most people were taking it easy on Christmas morning and sipping pre-lunch drinks, Campbell stared morosely through his binoculars at Coniston Water, as calm and peaceful as he had ever seen it. The temptation finally became too much for him. 'Come on,' he said to Paul and Anthony Robinson (two assistants), 'We're taking her out.' He went to tell Connie, who was in the kitchen cooking the Christmas turkey. 'All right Don', she said, 'But don't you dare be late back for lunch,' as if he had suggested slipping away to another pub for a lunchtime snifter. Donald did make sure that he was not late. It took him and his two assistants under an hour before they were back at the Sun, having had a completely satisfactory run up and down the lake. Donald never said exactly how fast he went, but it was generally believed to be in the region of 250 m.p.h. Though he had no time-keepers, no official observers, no press and no television cameras and an audience made up of mainly disinterested sheep, Donald brought back a good appetite for his Christmas turkey and plum pudding.

Two days later, it was fine again. This time skimming over

the placid water at an average speed of 280 m.p.h. Donald broke his record. But without timekeepers or observers, it just did not count. Of all the disappointments, this was the most frustrating of all.

This was the news which greeted the return of the team after Christmas. Once again the atmosphere was electrified with the kind of highly-charged feeling which Donald was capable of generating. He was now more certain than he had ever been that he had a new record and an excellent chance of the 300 m.p.h. plus in his pocket. The weather was bad again, but the Christmas break had shown just how quickly it could change for the better. It was now a race to see whether he would be given just that half an hour of calm water in the one hundred or so remaining before the New Year.

Rough water on Coniston delayed Donald Campbell's attempt to raise the world water speed record during the Christmas–New Year of 1966–7

But it was not to be, New Year's Day saw him anxiously waiting on the jetty hoping desperately for a break in the weather which seemed to be on the cards. He was on the point of deciding to launch *Bluebird* when a message came through over the radio that his official observers, the solicitor and friend Norman Buckley and Kendal businessman Andrew Brown, were unable to get to their positions at either end of the measured kilometre. The tourist cars were completely blocking all traffic.

Next day the weather was bad again and in the Sun Inn Donald held what was to be his last press conference. There was not a lot for him to say and few questions were left to be asked. During the nine weeks he had been there every possible aspect of the project had been discussed, not once but many times. There was no doubt that morale was again sinking when Tuesday, January 3, dawned wet and windy, and the south-west wind blew the clouds over Coniston Old Man, sweeping the lake into six-inch waves. Donald was hardly seen at all that day. For the first time there seemed to be a slight hint of inertia. There seemed to be an air of resignation about Donald, as though he realized that he could do no more than had been done, and the affair was now out of his hands and in the lap of the gods. He looked dreadfully tired. . . .

At a card game in the bungalow that night he drew the ace and the Queen of Spades, and told David Benson of the *Daily Express*: 'Mary Queen of Scots drew the same two cards the night before she was beheaded. I have the most awful premonition that I'm going to get the chop this time.'

Hound Trailing

New Year's Day is a most important date in the traditional Lake District sport of hound trailing, for this date is the 'official' birthday of all trail hound pups that are born during the year that follows. Although the pups are generally born during the months of January, February and March, January 1st is the key day, for this is the date of registration. All breeders must ensure that pups are registered within six weeks of birth, in order to be eligible to compete in official trails.

Hound trail pups aged about six weeks

During this six-week period, the pups will be earmarked with an individual identification number allocated by the Hound Trailing Association, which governs the sport in Cumbria.

Newly-registered pups will not, however, compete in trails until the season following that in which they were born. Pups born close to the registration date will have the edge on development over those pups born later in the season, when they come to start their competitive life the following year. Christmas time can be a period of tense expectancy for the breeders as they wait for the bitches to whelp. Will the power and strength of the stud dog blend with the quiet steadiness of the bitch? Will the genetic mix of a long line of ancestors produce a pup that will be strong enough, fast enough and brave enough to lead in a stream of other hounds in trail after trail over some of the roughest ground in the Lake District? Has the bitch's diet been correct? Will she be able to feed her own pups? Will she accept them? – are all questions that will only be answered after long weeks of waiting.

'What qualities are looked for in a pup?' I asked one breeder proudly showing off a litter of eight healthy pups.

'A dog that is bold but with a good temperament, with good bone structure, strong shoulders and legs, and big feet,' she told me. To the inexperienced eye, the pups look very much alike apart from the differing colour combinations of white, brown and black. But an old-time trailer can pick a pup out of a litter, and with a fair degree of accuracy, predict its future.

What lies in store for these New Year pups?

According to another breeder, 'a life of eating, sleeping, and running'. Once registered as a trail hound, it will follow the life style very similar to that of a finely-tuned athlete, to be trained to a state of peak fitness for its first trail.

A trail is laid over open country, usually fell or farm land, by dragging a cloth soaked in a mixture of aniseed and paraffin over a pre-determined distance. The mixture is made up to the official specification of the Hound Trailing Association. The distance is measured in time taken to run, rather than actual length, using the average speed of one mile every three minutes as the unit of measurement. The Hound Trailing Association was established in 1907, although much earlier records show that there were trails in which shepherds' dogs competed in the same race as the hound dogs. The trail hound is a different animal to the foxhound, being leaner and slimmer. Trail hounds are bred for speed, for a trail will last about twenty-five minutes, whereas foxhounds are bred for stamina, for they run for hours at a time while hunting over the Lakeland fells. Sometimes, a hound trail breeder will re-introduce the fox hound strain into his bloodline to improve the scenting qualities, for both types of hound evolved from the same stock.

Nowadays there are fifteen different categories of trail so that there is opportunity for a hound to be entered at a level most suited to the individual dog.

As trails are laid over open country, following a circular course, it is necessary to gain the consent and co-operation of many landowners, for fences have to be lowered, gates opened, and protection laid over barbed wire. It is in the main interest of hound trailing to ensure this agreement, for without it there would be no sport. One can appreciate the degree of co-operation needed, when it is realized that in the Lake District there are 300 organized meetings each session which involves the laying of over 1,000 trails.

Although hound trailing is a traditional Lakeland sport, it is not confined to this area, for it also takes place in the Borders, North Yorkshire, central areas of Wales and in parts of Ireland, where it is called 'drag hunting'. It is unusual for Cumbrian dogs to run outside their own area.

Breeders usually only keep one, or two dogs from a litter,

Trail hound breeder, Mrs Enid Taylor of Distington, with 'Buster'

the rest will be sold, and many of these go to owners in other areas anxious to introduce a fresh bloodline into their own stock. One could expect to pay between £50 and £100 for a pup from a good litter, but several hundreds of pounds for an adult dog of proven success.

The winter months is the time of the hound trailing 'close season' for trails are only laid between All Fool's Day or Easter Sunday (whichever is the sooner) and 31 October. This is the period when hounds and handlers can relax from racing after a busy season, although there is no relaxation for the breeders. The dogs have to be kept fit and this is achieved by many miles of daily walking. Hounds are always exercised on the lead for they are easily distracted, and if allowed to run loose, would probably follow any scent they came across. One trailer told me that that 'spoils a hound's nose'.

But during the long miles of hard road walking during winter months, handlers' eyes turn to the nearby fells, covered with fresh fallen snow, and see, in their minds, a line of tiny white dots racing across a green fell side; rippling through deep bracken, running over crag and scree with sure-footed jumps over wall and fence. The specks increase in size as handlers recognize their own and scream their names. Shrill whistles, waving arms, frantic flapping to urge them home. Muzzles into food bowls, gone in gulps, tails lash from side to side, panting, drooling with heaving flanks, in the renewed contact between dog, handler and food.

The frost rimed tarmac slides underfoot as the winter-coated hounds pad alongside their handlers in the frosty silence of a December morning. Who knows what champions will emerge as they step into the New Year?

The Ascent of Pillar Rock

A.G. GARDINER

No date is given for the writing of this account, but it would probably take place in the late nineteenth-century. Wasdale Head was the gathering point, at holiday times, for the men involved in the 'new' sport of rock climbing. In those early days, the men involved were mainly professional or university men who pioneered the routes on the great Lakeland crags.

Their equipment was cumbersome by modern day standards; guidebooks were still in the making, and for most of them, the actual feat of getting to Wasdale Head was a major task, involving a long walk up the valley from the railway station at Ravenglass, or Drigg. But in spite of the difficulties, these rock pioneers loved their mountains, and this article encapsulates the mood of camaraderie that developed among the rock climbing fraternity.

It is New Year's Day – clear and bright, patches of snow on the mountains and a touch of frost in the air. In the hall there is a mob of gay adventurers, tying up ropes, putting on puttees, filling rucksacks with provisions, hunting for boots (the boots are all alike, but you recognize them by your missing nails).

· A Lakes Christmas ·

We separate at the threshold – this group for the Great Gable, that for Scafell, ours, which includes George Abraham, for the Pillar Rock. It is a two and a half hours tramp thither by Black Sail Pass, and as daylight is short there is no time to waste. We follow the water course up the valley, splash through the marshes, faintly veneered with ice, cross the stream where the boulders give a decent foothold, and mount the steep ascent of Black Sail. From the top of the pass we look down lonely Ennerdale, where springing from the flank of the Pillar mountain, is the great Rock we have come to challenge. It stands like a tower, gloomy, impregnable, sheer, 600 feet

Climbing on Pillar Rock *c.* 1900

from its northern base to its summit, split on the south side by Jordan Gap that divides the High Man or main rock from Pisgah, the lesser rock. We have been overtaken by another party of three from the inn – one in a white jersey which, for reasons that will appear, I shall always remember. Together we follow the High Level Traverse, the track that leads round the flank of the mountain to the top of Walker's Gully, the grim descent to the valley, loved by the climber for the perils to which it invites him. Here we lunch and here we separate. We, unambitious (having three passengers in our party of five), are climbing the East Face by the Notch and Slab route; the others are ascending by the New West route, one of the more difficult climbs.

It is not of our climb I wish to speak, but of theirs. With five on the rope, however, our progress is slow, and it is two o'clock when we stand, first of the year, on the summit of Pillar Rock. We take a second lunch, and inscribe our names in the book that lies under the cairn, and then look down the precipice on the West face for signs of our late companions. The sound of their voices comes up from below but the drop is too sheer to catch a glimpse of their forms. 'They're going to be late,' says George Abraham, the discoverer of the New West – and then he indicates the closing stages of the climb. . . .

We descend by Slingsby's Crack and the Old West route which ends on a slope of the mountain near to the starting point of the New West route. The day is fading fast, and the moon that is rising in the East sheds no light on this face of the great tower. The voices now are quite distinct, coming to us from the left. 'Can't understand why those lads are cutting it so fine,' says George Abraham, and he hastens our pace down cracks and grooves and over ledges until we reach the screes and safety. And now we look up the great cliff and in the gathering dusk one thing is visible – a figure in a white jersey, with arms extended at full stretch. There it hangs minute by minute, as if nailed to the rocks.

'This is bad,' says George Abraham and he prepares for a possible emergency. 'Are you in difficulties? Shall we wait?' 'Yes wait,' the words rebound from the cliff in the still air like stones. We wait and watch. We can see nothing but the white jersey, still moveless; but every motion of the other climbers and every word they speak echoes down the precipice, as if from a sounding board. You hear the iron-shod feet of the climbers feeling for footholds on the ringing wall of rock. Once there is a horrible clatter as if both feet are dangling over the abyss and scraping convulsively for a hold. I fancy one or two of us feel a little uncomfortable as we look at each other in silent comment. And all the time the figure in white, now growing dim, is impaled on the face of darkness, and the voices come down to us in brief, staccato phrases. Above the rock, the moon is sailing into the clear winter sky and the stars are coming out.

At last the figure in white is seen to move and soon a cheery 'All right,' drops down from above. The difficult operation is over, nothing remains but the final slabs, which in the absence of ice offer no great difficulty. We turn to go with the comment that it is perhaps more sensational to watch a climb, than do one . . .

And we plunge over the debris behind Pisgah, climb up the Great Doup, where the snow lies crisp and deep, until we reach the friendly fence that has guided many a wanderer in the darkness down to the top of Black Sail Pass. From thence, the way is familiar, and two hours later we have rejoined the merry party round the board at the inn.

In a few days it is all over. This one back in the Temple, that one to his office, a third to his pulpit, another to his mill, and all seem prosaic and ordinary. But they will carry with them a secret music. Say only the word 'Wastdale' to them and you shall awake its echoes; then you shall see their faces light up with the emotion of incommunicable things. They are no longer men of the world; they are spirits of the mountains.

Acknowledgements

'The Twelve Days of Yule' by Dorothy Una Ratcliffe published in *Cumbria* magazine, December 1981, and is reprinted with acknowledgement to the author. Extracts from *Fellwanderer*, *Ex-Fellwanderer*, Volume Seven of the Pictorial Guides *The Western Fells*, all by A. Wainwright, are reproduced with the permission of the author and the copyright holder, the *Westmorland Gazette*. Extracts from *Months at the Lakes* by Canon H.D. Rawnsley (1906), published by James Maclehose & Sons. Extracts from the Wasdale Head Inn Visitors Books 1879 – 94, reprinted with permission of the County Record Office (Kendal), Fell and Rock Climbing Club (ref WDSo/163). *Christmas as an Evacuee* by Joan Mullen is reprinted by permission of the author. Extracts from *To the King's Deceit* by Ronald T Gibbon (1983), reprinted by permission of the Friends of Whitehaven Museum with acknowledgement to the author. 'The Aircraft and Father Christmas' (1926) is reprinted by permission of the *Westmorland Gazette Newspapers*. Extracts from *Letters of William Wordsworth* edited by Alan G. Gill (1984) and reprinted by permission of Oxford University Press. Extract from *Confessions of an Opium Eater* by Thomas de Quincey (1821), was included in *A Collection of the Works of Thomas de Quincey*, edited by J.T. Fields, published by Tinkner, Reed and Fields, Boston 1851. Extracts from *Tom Rumney of Mellfell* by A.W. Rumney (1936), published by Titus Wilson, Kendal and reprinted with acknowledgement to the author. *Christmas on the La' al Ratty* by Ian and Gillian Stanistreet is reprinted by permission of the authors. *Christmas in Company* by Evelyn Adams MBE is reprinted by permission of the author. 'Don't drink and drive' is reprinted with acknowledgement to the *Whitehaven News*, 22nd December, 1898. Extracts from *Wandering in Lakeland* by W.T. Palmer (1946), published by Skivington, is reprinted with acknowledgement to the author and publisher. Extracts from *Elizabethan Keswick* by W.G. Collingwood (1912) and published by Titus Wilson, Kendal. *Down at the Mill* by Pat Evans is reprinted by permission of the author. Extracts from *Inside the Real Lakeland* by A.H. Griffin (1961), published by the Guardian Press and reprinted by permission of the author. Extracts from *From the Other Side of the Bar* by Florence Bradley (1981), published by New Horizon, and reprinted with the permission of the author. Extracts from *Bygone Cumberland and Westmorland* by Daniel Scott (1899), published by William Andrews. Extract from *Rogue Herries* by Sir Hugh Walpole (1930), published by MacMillan, is reprinted by permission of the publisher. 'Nature Notes' December 1926 is reprinted by permission of the *Westmorland Gazette Newspapers*. 'Miracle in the Marketplace' by Carson I.A. Ritchie, published in *Cumbria* magazine, December 1989, and reprinted with permission of the author. 'The Snow' by John Richardson, (1874) and reprinted from *Cumberland Mak o' Talk*. Extract from *A Christmas Party* is reprinted from Suart's Almanack, December 1896. 'The Shape of Gifts to Come' by Barry Knowles, published in *Cumbria* magazine, October 1989, and reprinted by permission of the author. 'Christmas Weather' is reprinted from parish records of Watermillock 1607. Extract from *History of Cumbria* by W.M. Hutchinson (1796). Extract from *The Verge of Lakeland* by W.T. Palmer (1938), published by Robert Hale, is reprinted by permission of the publisher. Extracts from *Dorothy Wordsworth's Grasmere Journals* edited by William Knight (1904) and published by MacMillan, reprinted with acknowledgement to the publisher. 'Logs to Burn'; traditional is from *A Field Guide to the Lake District*

173

· A Lakes Christmas ·

by Jim Taylor Page, published by Dalesman Publishing Co (1984), and reprinted by permission of the author. Extracts from *Lakeland and the Borders of Long Ago* by Walter MacIntire (1949) published by the *Cumbrian News*, and reprinted by permission of the publishers, with acknowledgement to Cumbrian Newspapers Limited. Extracts from *Mountain Lakeland* by Tom Bowker (1983), published by Robert Hale, and reprinted with the permission of the author and publisher. 'The Christmas Carol' is reprinted from the parish magazine of St Michaels, Workington, December, 1903. 'The Other Side of the Altar' by Howard Askew is reprinted with permission of the author. Boggles by the Reverend J. Bulkeley (1885), is reprinted from the Transactions of the Cumberland and Westmorland Archaeological and Antiquarian Society. Extract from *Christmas in a Fellside Community* by Barbara Smith was published in *Cumbria* magazine, December 1973, and is reprinted with acknowledgement to the author. Extract from 'Mountain Rescues Recalled' by 'Sally Bowe' (1987), published by the *Westmorland Gazette*, is reprinted by permission of the author and publisher. Extract from *Donald Campbell* by Douglas Young-James (1960), published by Neville Spearman, is reprinted with acknowledgement to the author. 'The Ascent of Pillar Rock' by A.G. Gardiner was published in *Prose and Poetry of Cumbria* edited by Walter and Claire Jerrold (1930), and is reprinted with acknowledgement to the copyright holder.

Picture Credits

Abbot Hall Museum of Lakeland Life and Industry, Kendal, pp. 26, 75, 76, 83, 84, 89, 94, 109, 120, 154, 162; Abraham Brothers, Keswick, pp. 2, 3, 12, 88, 169; Howard Askew, original drawings, pp. 69, 100; Fell and Rock Climbing Club and the County Record Office, Kendal – Wasdale Head Visitors' Book 1892–94. ref WDSo/163, pp. 17, 21; Fishers, London, engravings by Thomas Allan and George Pickering, pp. 51, 126; Friends of Whitehaven Museum, pp. 28, 54, 91; Kendal County Museum, pp. 72, 129, 131, 133; Barry Knowles, original cartoons, pp. 114–119; Ravenglass and Eskdale Railway Preservation Society, pp. 55, 57, 60; B. Richardson, p. 15; Frank Robinson, from *Tales of Father Christmas*, 1906, pp. 49, 124; West Cumberland Times and Star, p. 8.
All other photographs by the compiler.